Get Ready! for Social Stud[...]
ESSAYS, BOOK REPORTS, AND RESEARCH PAPERS

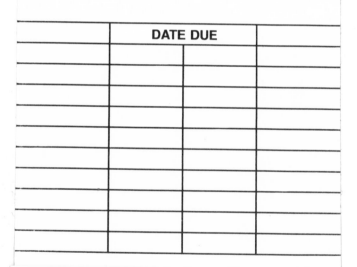

	DATE DUE		

Books in the *Get Ready! for Social Studies* Series:

Essays, Book Reports, and Research Papers
Geography
Government and Citizenship
U.S. History
World History

Nancy White and Francine Weinberg, series editors, have been involved in educating elementary and secondary students for more than thirty years. They have had experience in the classroom as well as on dozens of books and electronic projects. They welcome this partnership with parents and other adults to promote knowledge, skills, and critical thinking.

Get Ready! for Social Studies
ESSAYS, BOOK REPORTS, AND RESEARCH PAPERS

Nancy White
Francine Weinberg

McGraw-Hill
New York   Chicago   San Francisco
Lisbon   London   Madrid   Mexico City
Milan   New Delhi   San Juan   Seoul
Singapore   Sydney   Toronto

Library of Congress Cataloging-in-Publication Data applied for.

McGraw-Hill

A Division of The McGraw·Hill Companies

1 2 3 4 5 6 7 8 9 0   QPD/QPD   0 9 8 7 6 5 4 3 2

ISBN 0-07-137759-X

This book was set in Goudy Oldstyle by North Market Street Graphics.

Printed and bound by Quebecor/Dubuque.

McGraw-Hill books are available at special quantity discounts to use as premiums and sales promotions, or for use in corporate training programs. For more information, please write to the Director of Special Sales, Professional Publishing, McGraw-Hill, Two Penn Plaza, New York, NY 10121-2298. Or contact your local bookstore.

 This book is printed on recycled, acid-free paper containing a minimum of 50% recycled, de-inked fiber.

Contents

Introduction

In recent years, the media have told us that many students need to improve their writing skills. Many parents and other adults like you find themselves looking for ways to help students who bring home assignments to write paragraphs, essays, book reports, and full-scale research papers. Students need help in budgeting their time, getting started, seeing the task through, and knowing how to judge their own work. *Essays, Book Reports, and Research Papers* provides step-by-step instruction, models for different kinds of writing, and practical aids for actually completing their assignments.

You may choose to use this book in several different ways, depending on your child's strengths and preferences. You might read passages aloud; you might read it to yourself and then paraphrase it for your child; or you might ask your child to read the material along with you or on his or her own. To help you use this book successfully, brief boldface paragraphs, addressed to you, the adult, appear from time to time. In addition, key terms appear in boldface type throughout the text.

Here is a preview of the features you will find in each chapter:

What Your Child Needs to Know

This section provides practical strategies and techniques students can use to complete their assignments and improve their writing.

Implications

This section gives you answers to questions many students ask themselves about writing in general: Why is writing important in the first place? How am I ever going to get through this? What can I do to get a better grade?

Skills Practice

These exercises are more than just practice. When your child completes them, he or she will be a step closer to having a completed product to hand in.

Top of the Class

In this section, creative suggestions help students stand out in class. By taking some of these suggestions, students can show their teachers that they have been putting in the extra effort that means the difference between average and excellent performance.

Don't forget the helpful material at the back of the book.

Writer's Handbook

This section includes useful facts and documents that your child can access quickly and easily while writing about social studies and other subjects.

The book you are now holding in your hand is a powerful tool. It will help you boost your child's performance in school, increase his or her self-confidence, and open the door to a successful future as a well-educated adult.

Nancy White and Francine Weinberg

CHAPTER 1
Paragraphs and Essays

What Your Child Needs to Know

You may choose to use the following text in several different ways, depending on your child's strengths and preferences. You might read passages aloud; you might read them to yourself and then paraphrase them for your child; or you might ask your child to read the material along with you or on his or her own.

In social studies, language arts, science, and other subjects, teachers are placing more and more emphasis on student writing. Educators have long recognized that a piece of writing is better than a short-answer test as an indicator of whether students have learned and understood specific subject matter. Even more important is the growing awareness that the ability to communicate ideas in a meaningful, well-organized way is an essential skill for success throughout life—not only in school. Therefore, it is very likely that elementary- and middle-school children will be coming home with assignments to write a paragraph or essay.

Many students' hearts sink when they hear they have a writing assignment for homework, but writing a paragraph or an essay does not have to be a daunting challenge. This chapter is designed to help guide a child through the process of producing a well-written paragraph or essay. By becoming familiar with a sequence of steps to follow from the initial planning stages to the final product, any child will find that he or she can approach a writing assignment with confidence rather than trepidation.

WHEN THE ASSIGNMENT GIVES THE TOPIC AND ASKS FOR ONLY A PARAGRAPH

A homework assignment or an essay question on a test may call for a response that is only one **paragraph** long. The teacher usually asks for a paragraph in order to determine whether students can recall facts about a **topic,** understand concepts, and express the ideas in their own words—or whether students need more help. The assumption behind such an assignment or test question is that the students have read assigned material and/or have participated in whole-class or small-group discussions about the topic. That is, students will not be doing any other reading or research in order to respond to the writing assignment. (Educators sometimes call the assignment a **writing prompt.)**

Here are examples of such assignments from a leading social studies textbook.

- Write a paragraph describing the three branches of the U.S. government.
- Write a paragraph explaining how your climate is affected by three factors: distance from the equator, elevation above sea level, and distance from the ocean.
- Write a paragraph that compares and contrasts Navajo daily life in the 1600s with Navajo life today.

Let's see how a student can go about responding to Paragraph Assignment 1.

Clarifying What the Paragraph Should Contain

Few school projects cause more frustration than putting a lot of work into a piece of writing and then hearing the teacher say that the piece is not what the assignment asked for. For generations now, teachers have advised students to read each and every assignment very closely, maybe even to underline its key, or most important, words.

Reading carefully, we see that Paragraph Assignment 1 calls for a paragraph that describes something. *Describes* means "creates a picture of something in words." So a description can tell how something appears to the senses (how it looks, smells, sounds, and so on), or a description can identify the parts of something and explain their functions. What does Paragraph Assignment 1 ask the writer to identify and tell about the parts of? The three branches of the U.S. government. The writer who "translated" the assignment this way is off to a good start.

Planning a Paragraph

Should the student now begin writing his or her paragraph? No. He or she should start by **planning** the paragraph. In times past, jotting down notes and ideas on scratch paper was all that planning involved. Today, many textbooks and teachers say that planning is part of something larger called **prewriting.**

Two of the most effective tools for planning a paragraph (or most other pieces of writing) are a **list** and a **graphic organizer.** The latter is simply a fancy name for a diagram that helps the writer to keep track of what he or she knows and to decide how to organize those facts and ideas—what to put first, what to put second, and so on. Paragraph Assignment 1 asks for a description of three things, so a writer would be wise to create a graphic organizer with three parts— maybe three circles or three columns—and to label each with the name of a branch of the U.S. government. Then, under each label, the writer should jot down everything he or she can remember about the branch, even though some of that information may not end up in the actual paragraph. Here's an example of a chart that shows a student's planning for Paragraph Assignment 1.

TOPIC OF PARAGRAPH: DESCRIPTION OF THREE BRANCHES OF U.S. GOVERNMENT		
Judicial	Legislative	Executive
• Makes decisions about laws • Decides whether laws are constitutional • Decides whether people are guilty of federal crimes • Federal judges appointed by the president	• Makes laws • Congress—Senate and House of Representatives • How a bill is passed in both houses • Possible veto by president • Possible override of veto	• Includes president, vice president • Includes cabinet, Executive Office of the President, agencies • President has many jobs including chief executive and commander in chief of the armed forces
③	②	①

After writing notes in the columns, the writer must think about which branch of government to discuss first, which second, and which third. The numerals at the bottom of each column show a writer's decision to discuss the executive branch first. In some cases, a writer might decide to present information in **chronological order,** in **order of importance,** or, if describing something visually, in **spatial order.** In this case, the writer may have simply decided to present the three branches of the federal government in the order used in his or her social studies textbook.

Drafting a Topic Sentence and the Supporting Details

Either before or after jotting down the notes, the writer needs to think about a topic sentence. A **topic sentence** helps the reader understand what all the other sentences in a paragraph add up to. In other words, the topic sentence is a general statement, and every other sentence in the paragraph should, in some way, add **details** to or **support** that statement.

Not all paragraphs have topic sentences, but topic sentences help young writers—and readers of young writers—a lot. In general, students need to become more advanced writers before they can write a well-constructed paragraph without a topic sentence.

Here are a couple of topic sentences that a writer could use to begin a paragraph describing the three branches of the U.S. government.

> *The three branches of the United States government are the executive branch, the legislative branch, and the judicial branch.*
>
> *The United States government is divided into three branches—the executive, the legislative, and the judicial.*

With a topic sentence and the three-column graphic organizer, a student should find starting to write in response to Paragraph Assignment 1 a little easier than if he or she tried to start "cold."

The next step is to transform the notes in the graphic organizer, along with the topic sentence, into a **first draft** of a paragraph. This step involves making some choices. After all, the assignment asks the student to write only one paragraph, so the student won't have room to include *everything* he or she has learned in social studies class about the three branches of the U.S. government. The writer may make decisions about what to include and what to exclude before drafting or while drafting.

No one expects a draft to be perfect. In fact, the noun *draft* means "a first rough copy." With this definition in mind, along with the knowledge that no one has to see a first draft except the writer, a child will be able to get started without feeling nervous about making mistakes or writing something that sounds "dumb." Later, this chapter will say more about eliminating errors in drafts and making other changes to improve them. For the time being, let's look at a first draft that grew out of the planning, or prewriting, notes about the U.S. government.

> *The United States government is divided into three branches—the executive, the legislative, and the judicial. The executive branch include the president, the vice president, the president's cabinet, the Executive Office of the President, and*

many federal agencies. Examples of federal agencies are the Environmental Protection Agency and the U.S. Post Office. There are many federal agencies. The purpose of the executive branch is to enforce the laws of our country. The legislative branch is made up of the Senate and the House of Representatives, which are the two houses of Congress. The branches' purpose is to make laws for our country. It's important for every country to have laws. The judicial branch is made up of federal judges. These judges make decisions about whether laws are constitutional. They are apointed by the president. They also preside over trials for federal crimes.

A couple of comments about the sample paragraph: first, the topic sentence is at the very beginning of the sample, but not every paragraph puts the topic sentence first. Sometimes the topic sentence comes in the middle or at the end of a paragraph. (Later in this chapter, we'll show an example of a paragraph with the topic sentence at the end.) Second, the sample paragraph is not perfect. But before we show how to fix a paragraph, let's go on to look at an assignment that calls for writing *more* than one paragraph.

WHEN THE ASSIGNMENT GIVES THE TOPIC AND ASKS FOR AN ESSAY

At a certain point, teachers want students to write more than a single paragraph. They will expect an essay, which consists of several paragraphs. Whether teachers use the term **essay** or **composition** or **paper** or **article** or **theme,** they are asking for a multiparagraph piece of writing. Here are examples of essay assignments from a leading social studies textbook.

- Write a short essay (no less than 500 words) about Islam as one of the world's major religions. What are its main beliefs and practices?
- Suppose you are a television reporter sent back in time to ancient Rome to cover the assassination of Julius Caesar. Write a report that you will give on the evening news.
- Write a newspaper article in which you describe one of the Revolutionary War battles you have read about in this chapter. Include dates, events, and people who played key roles in the battle. Write a headline for your article.

We'll look at how a student might respond to Essay Assignment 1.

Clarifying What the Essay Should Contain

Reading carefully, we see that Essay Assignment 1 asks the writer to think about the topic Islam, which is defined as a major world religion, and to write about two **subtopics**—(a) beliefs of Muslims and (b) practices of Muslims.

Planning the Essay: The Body, the Introduction, and the Conclusion

Just as with the paragraph-writing assignment, the student should *not* immediately jump into writing the essay sentence by sentence. First, he or she should plan what to say about (a) beliefs of Muslims and (b) practices of Muslims. To start the planning, or prewriting, phase, the student could set up a graphic organizer—a two-column chart, with one column headed "Beliefs" and one column, "Practices."

TOPIC: ISLAM, A MAJOR WORLD RELIGION	
Beliefs of Muslims	*Practices of Muslims*
Only one God, like Christians and Jews.	*Five Pillars of Islam (duties of Muslims)*
Allah is same God worshiped by Christians and Jews.	*1. State "there is only one God" and agree that Muhammad was his messenger.*
Muhammad is a prophet, like Moses in the Bible.	*2. Give money to the poor.*
Koran is Muslim holy book with words God spoke to Muhammad in 600s.	*3. Pray 5 times a day. (Wash before praying. Stand, bow, kneel, lie down.)*
Muhammad got God's messages from the angel Gabriel.	*4. Fast in daytime during month of Ramadan (ninth month of Muslim year).*
Afterlife—heaven and hell.	*5. Travel to Mecca to pray. (Muhammad was born in Mecca.) Wear special clothes on journey.*
Children born without sin.	*Customs Feast after Ramadan is over.*
	Party when boy or girl memorizes large section of Koran.
	Things Muslims cannot do Eat pork. Drink alcohol.

With so many notes, the student should do two things before beginning to write.

1. The student should convert the notes into an easy-to-follow **outline** for the **body,** or main part, of the report. The outline should also show that the student will include an opening paragraph, or **introduction,** as well as a final paragraph, or **conclusion.**
2. The student must write a special opening sentence for the introduction. The special sentence is called a **thesis statement.**

The student can do these two things in either order: the outline and then the thesis statement or the thesis statement and then the outline. Here is an outline that a student could have written using the notes in the preceding chart.

INTRODUCTION

A. BELIEFS OF ISLAM

Muslims believe in only one God (Allah).

Allah is the same God worshiped by Christians and Jews.

In 600s, Muhammad got God's messages from angel Gabriel.

Koran is book with words God spoke to Muhammad through Gabriel.

B. PRACTICES OF ISLAM

Five Pillars (Duties)

- *State "there is only one God" and agree that Muhammad was his messenger.*
- *Pray 5 times a day. Wash before praying. Stand, bow, kneel, lie down.*
- *Give money to the poor.*
- *Fast in daytime during month of Ramadan.*
- *Go to Mecca in Saudi Arabia to pray. (Muhammad was born in Mecca.) Wear special clothes on journey.*

Other Rules

- *No eating pork.*
- *No drinking alcohol.*

Customs

- *Feast after Ramadan.*
- *Party when boy or girl memorizes large part of Koran.*

CONCLUSION

Notice these things about the outline:

- The student has used capital letters and underlining to indicate main topics and subtopics. (Students may have learned to use the more complicated system of Roman numerals and Arabic numerals and capital and lowercase letters for an outline. Students should follow their teacher's advice, but we recommend this easier system of outlining.)
- Some notes didn't make it into the outline. As when writing a single paragraph, a writer doesn't have to use all his or her notes; it's fine—probably even necessary—to leave some out. On the other hand, sometimes a writer adds another piece of information to an outline—a detail that didn't appear on the original notes but that the writer thought of later.
- On the outline, the writer changed the order of some of the notes—to put related subtopics closer together. That's fine, too.
- Each capitalized or underlined term can become its own paragraph. So this outline can lead to four body paragraphs plus an introductory paragraph and a concluding paragraph—six paragraphs in all. Students should remember that a paragraph cannot be just one sentence. If a writer has nothing more to say about a topic, he or she should incorporate that sentence into another paragraph or should leave it out altogether.

Now would be a good time for the student to figure out what he or she will write as the introduction and the conclusion for the essay. An effective introduction will let the reader know what the essay is about. The opening sentence, or thesis statement, should succinctly state the **main idea** of the essay, and one or two additional sentences should elaborate or clarify the main idea. Here's a possible introduction for the essay on Islam. Notice how the first sentence—the thesis statement—picks up and reuses words from the assignment. Also notice the follow-up sentence after the thesis statement.

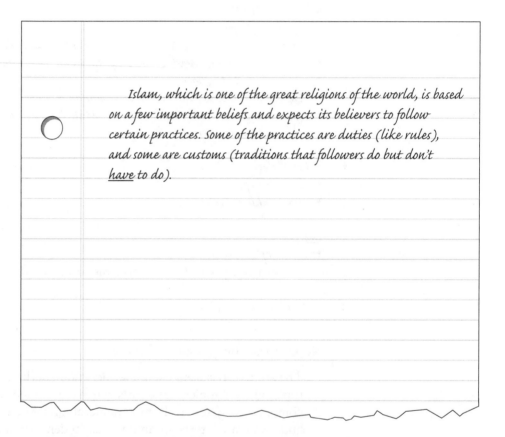

Islam, which is one of the great religions of the world, is based on a few important beliefs and expects its believers to follow certain practices. Some of the practices are duties (like rules), and some are customs (traditions that followers do but don't have to do).

The introduction to an essay is important because the thesis statement works as the overview for the whole essay, and the topic sentence for each body paragraph relates to, adds details to, or supports the thesis statement. If, in turn, every sentence in each paragraph adds details to or supports the topic sentence of that paragraph, the writer will end up with a nicely organized, easy-to-follow essay.

As far as the conclusion goes, a writer has a few choices. He or she can write a summary of the material in the body (this is okay but can be boring and sound repetitive) or offer a fresh idea for the reader to take away from the essay. If choosing the latter, however, the writer should be careful not to introduce a completely new and unrelated idea that "comes out of the blue" and has no backup or support from the body of the essay.

Here is the complete essay. Remember that it's only a first draft, so it has problems and errors that we will deal with later on.

The thesis statement at the beginning of the essay states the main idea of the essay.

The topic sentence at the beginning of this paragraph relates to the thesis statement by mentioning *beliefs*.

The topic sentence at the beginning of this paragraph supports the thesis statement by mentioning *practices* of Islam.

This topic sentence comes at the end of the paragraph rather than at the beginning. It supports the thesis statement by mentioning *rules*.

The topic sentence at the beginning of this paragraph supports the thesis statement by mentioning *customs*.

Islam, which is one of the great religions of the world, is based on a few important beliefs and expects its believers to follow certain practices. Some of the practices are duties (like rules), and some are customs (traditions that followers do but don't have to do).

The beliefs of Islam are mostly about God and about Muhammad, who brought the words of God to the Muslim people. Like Christians and Jews, they believe in only one God. Muslims believe that God sent the angel Gabriel to bring God's messages to a man named Muhammad in the 600s. The words God spoke to Muhammad through Gabriel is written down in the Muslim holy book, called the Koran. Their God, called Allah, is the same God worshiped by Christians and Jews.

Muslims practice their religion by doing certain duties that they have to do. These duties are called the Five Pillars of Islam. The first is to state "there is only one God" and agree that Muhammad was his messenger. The second is to pray five times a day. Muslims must wash before praying, and at different times during their prayers they must stand, bow, kneel, and lie down. The third duty is to give money to the poor. The fourth is to fast in the daytime during Ramadan. Ramadan is the nineth month of the Muslim year. The fifth duty is to travel to Mecca to pray. Mecca is a holy city for Muslims because Muhammad was born there.

Muslims must not eat pork and they must not ever drink alcohol. These are rules, too, but they tell people what they must not do instead of what they must do.

Muslims also practice their religion by following certain customs. They don't have to do these things, but most Muslims do them. Examples of Muslim customs are feasting after Ramadan is over and having a big party in honor of a boy or girl who has memorized a large section of the Koran.

Islam is one of the world's newer religions. It started hundreds of years after Christianity and thousands of years after Judaism. Yet, with more than a billion followers, it has become one of the great religions of the world.

Notice that, in the conclusion, this student summarized by repeating that Islam is one of the world's great religions but added new information—the number of Muslims in the world today. The conclusion also adds a fresh idea by stressing that Islam is a relatively new religion.

GIVING THE PARAGRAPH OR ESSAY A TITLE

Although the **title** is the first thing the reader of a paragraph or essay sees, it's probably the last thing the writer should add. Sometimes coming up with a good title before beginning to write is difficult, but ideas often come to mind while the actual writing is going on. A good title should not be too long. It should let the reader know what the paragraph or essay is about, and it's a plus if the title can capture the reader's interest. But students shouldn't get bogged down in struggling to make a title overly clever or cute. A fine title for the student's essay on Islam, for example, would be "The Beliefs and Practices of Islam," "Islam: Beliefs and Practices," or "The Religion of the Muslim People."

Before we go on to look at how to improve first drafts of paragraphs and essays, let's consider one other situation students sometimes find themselves in.

WHEN THE ASSIGNMENT LEAVES THE TOPIC UP TO THE STUDENT

Some teachers want to give students practice not only in writing a paragraph or an essay in response to a specified topic; these teachers want to challenge students to come up with a topic by themselves. Such teachers may limit the students to the subject matter they have just studied together as a class, but within that limitation the students' choices are wide open. Here are a couple examples of such assignments:

1. Select an event from the Civil War, and write 200 words about it.
2. Write an essay telling which biome, or natural region, of the world you would prefer to live in and why. (The biomes are desert, forest, grassland, polar region, mountain, ocean, wetland.)

How should a student facing such assignments begin? Let's follow the process of a student who must do Open Assignment 1.

Ways to Narrow a Topic

At this point, the writer has to (1) **narrow down** a broad topic—such as the Civil War, (2) figure out a main point (another name for a thesis statement) about the narrowed topic, and (3) support the main point with details. To do all this, the writer can use one or more of many related methods, including the following: brainstorming, freewriting, and clustering. All the methods generate results in ten to fifteen minutes, and all the methods give thinkers permission to not worry about spelling, punctuation, or grammar and usage at this stage (as long as the thinkers can read back their notes!).

Brainstorming is basically list making. When people first start listing ideas about X (in our case, X equals the Civil War), they tend to think of the obvious. After a while, though, more original and creative ideas start to occur to brainstormers. The key is not to censor oneself at all but to list as many X-related ideas as possible, remembering that no one will see or judge the list. Often, just when a writer thinks he or she has run out of ideas, the brain kicks out a few more. Here's an example of brainstorming engaged in by somebody who had to decide on one event of the Civil War to write about.

Gettysburg
Other battles
Sherman burning Atlanta
Election of Abraham Lincoln
Emancipation Proclamation
Beginning: Fort Sumter
End: Appomattox ****
   I'll choose Appomattox. In 200 words, I can write about
   Who? (what Lee and Grant said, what they looked like)
   Why? (Why didn't Lee keep trying to win?)
   When? (few weeks before Lincoln's murder)
   What happened to guns and horses after surrender?

Freewriting takes the form of running prose instead of a list and requires the writer not to stop writing even if he or she can't think of anything else to say. Here's an example of what the "don't stop" rule may produce when someone is trying to narrow down the Civil War to one event to write about.

> One event. Oh, I can think of them but how will I know which one to pick? Everyone is going to write about the Gettysburg Address, I bet. I don't want to write about what everyone else writes about. Let's see: Maybe I should write about the battle of Gettysburg. I don't know enough about that either. I need something that's not a battle. Not a battle. Not a battle. I'll write about the surrender— when Lee had to surrender to Grant. I think I remember enough about that: where it was, when it was, what they looked like, who said what, what they signed, what happened after they signed the papers. OK!

Clustering (which is sometimes called **mapping** and sometimes **webbing**) is more visual than either brainstorming or freewriting. The writer puts the subject, such as "Events of the Civil War," in a circle in the middle of a blank page. Next, the writer thinks of examples or details and puts them in smaller circles of their own, attached to the central circle. The writer can then focus on one of the examples or details and draw additional circles around it with yet more specific examples and more specific details. Here's an example of a cluster generated by a student who was given the assignment to write an essay about a Civil War event.

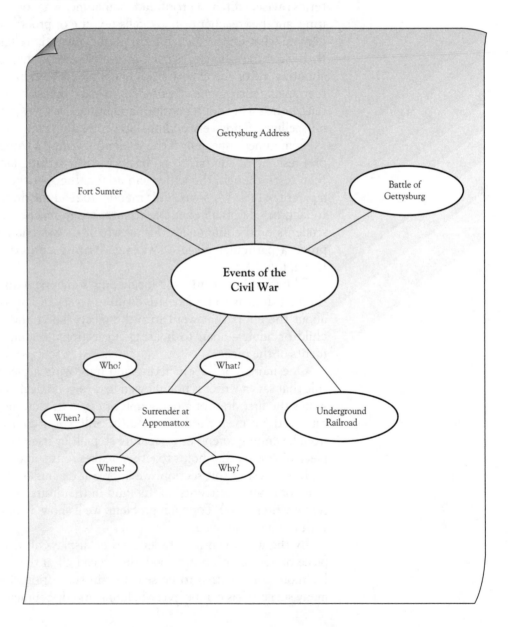

Once the brainstorming, freewriting, or mapping is over, the student who has to come up with a topic can proceed, like the student who wrote the essay on Islam did, to prepare an outline and a draft, including a thesis statement, introduction, body of the essay, conclusion, and title.

TROUBLESHOOTING: IMPROVING THE PIECE OF WRITING AND REMOVING ERRORS

Having drafted a paragraph or an essay, many writers would consider their job finished. After all, they've written what the assignment called for. But the truth of the matter is that just about every single piece that someone writes (with the possible exception of a shopping list) can get better when the writer goes back over it to revise it, edit it, proofread it, or all three. Let's also acknowledge that teachers and textbooks don't all attach the same meaning to each of the three terms **revise, edit,** and **proofread.** Sometimes what one teacher or book calls editing, another teacher or book calls revising or proofreading. So we won't insist here on what we think each term means. Instead, we'll just state loud and clear that when the writer goes back over a piece of writing and engages in **troubleshooting,** he or she almost always improves it both in big ways (for example, by rearranging paragraphs or sentences to make the flow clearer, by adding more details, or by taking out repetition) and in smaller ways (for example, by correcting misspellings, fixing verb endings, and correcting punctuation).

Sometimes, especially if the student is writing a paragraph or an essay as part of a test, he or she has to go back over the writing alone. In situations other than tests, though, the writer can ask another person—a teacher, a classmate, a parent, a relative, or an adult friend—to read the draft and provide **feedback.** In fact, in schools all over the country today, teachers and students or pairs of students hold conferences during which they exchange ideas on how to improve a particular piece of writing. **Writing conferences** can take place at home, too.

The most important rule for helping someone with his or her writing after the first draft is to find positive things to say about aspects of the work and about the effort that went into the piece. Then and only then is a writer—child or adult—open to hearing suggestions for improving one or two elements of the piece.

One more word about fixing and improving a piece of writing: there's no rule that says a writer is not allowed to do a good deal of self-editing as he or she writes the first draft of a paragraph or essay. In fact, most writers do this naturally, without even thinking about it. Still, going over the entire draft to fix it from beginning to end as a separate step all by itself is essential to producing a piece of writing that holds together, makes sense, and reads well.

In the rest of this section, we'll look at examples of five common problems that come up in students' drafts (and in the drafts of older people and professional writers, too). For each problem, we'll show a second version of the piece with the problem fixed.

By the way, even if a student writer displays all five problems in the same piece of writing, it's not a good idea to call all of them to his or her attention. It's more constructive to be selective in suggestions for improvement, as too many suggestions can be overwhelming and discouraging.

Common Problem 1: Not Enough Supporting Details

A paragraph makes a general point, which is usually stated in the topic sentence. A successful paragraph needs to provide enough details to support, or back up, that point. Here is part of a paragraph a student wrote in response to the following assignment:

> Write an essay telling which biome, or natural region, of the world you would prefer to live in and why. (The biomes are desert, forest, grassland, polar region, mountain, ocean, wetland.)

The following paragraph is weak because it does not provide enough supporting detail.

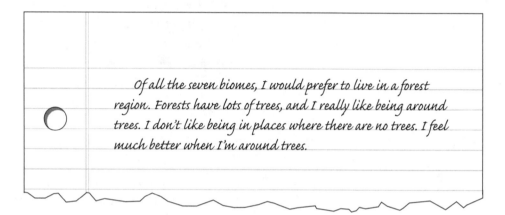

Of all the seven biomes, I would prefer to live in a forest region. Forests have lots of trees, and I really like being around trees. I don't like being in places where there are no trees. I feel much better when I'm around trees.

The topic sentence is acceptable, but the following sentences do not provide enough detail to back it up. The writer just keeps repeating the same idea. Here's what the paragraph might look like after the writer identifies its problem and fixes it:

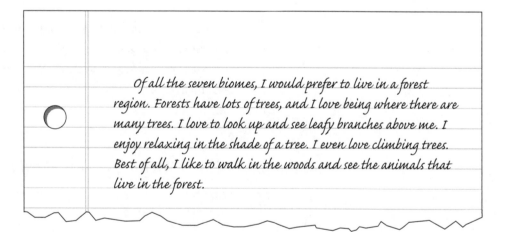

Of all the seven biomes, I would prefer to live in a forest region. Forests have lots of trees, and I love being where there are many trees. I love to look up and see leafy branches above me. I enjoy relaxing in the shade of a tree. I even love climbing trees. Best of all, I like to walk in the woods and see the animals that live in the forest.

Common Problem 2: Details That Don't Belong

While it is important that a paragraph give the reader enough details, it's just as important to keep unnecessary or irrelevant details out of a paragraph. They just distract and confuse the reader. In other words, "the more the better" doesn't alays work as a writer's motto. Here is part of a paragraph that includes details that do not belong. It was written in response to this assignment:

Write a paragraph that compares and contrasts Navajo daily life in the 1600s with Navajo life today.

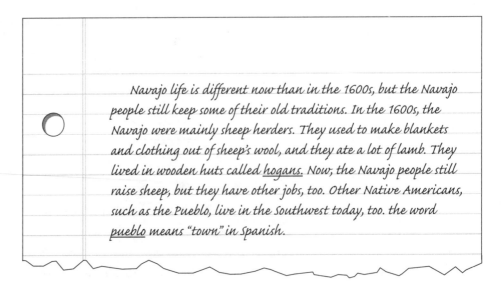

Navajo life is different now than in the 1600s, but the Navajo people still keep some of their old traditions. In the 1600s, the Navajo were mainly sheep herders. They used to make blankets and clothing out of sheep's wool, and they ate a lot of lamb. They lived in wooden huts called <u>hogans</u>. Now, the Navajo people still raise sheep, but they have other jobs, too. Other Native Americans, such as the Pueblo, live in the Southwest today, too. the word <u>pueblo</u> means "town" in Spanish.

The sample paragraph lacks **unity.** In other words, it doesn't stick to one topic. The last two sentences, beginning with "Other Native Americans . . . ," may be interesting, but they are off the topic. They have to go. As replacements for them, the student could add the following:

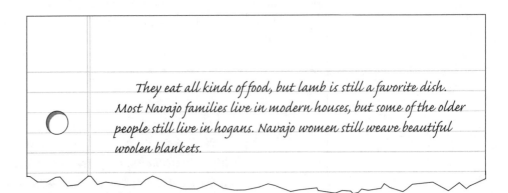

They eat all kinds of food, but lamb is still a favorite dish. Most Navajo families live in modern houses, but some of the older people still live in hogans. Navajo women still weave beautiful woolen blankets.

Common Problem 3: Writing That Is Hard to Follow

A good writer knows how to make a piece of writing easy for the reader to follow. Here are a few ways to do this.

- **Use transitions.** A thoughtful writer leads the reader from one idea to the next with words and phrases such as "Next," "Another reason is that . . . ," "Although . . . ," and "However."
- **Put information in a sensible order.** For example, when writing about an event, an effective writer gives each detail in **chronological,** or time, order. If a writer mentions details out of order, the reader will get lost.
- **Keep promises.** Readers get annoyed with a writer who writes, "Julius Caesar was assassinated for three reasons," then gives only two reasons.

In the following example (part of a paragraph from an essay about the assassination of Julius Caesar), the writer neglected transitions. The writing sounds choppy and is hard to follow.

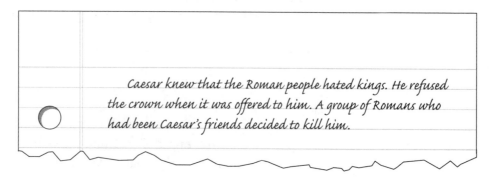

Caesar knew that the Roman people hated kings. He refused the crown when it was offered to him. A group of Romans who had been Caesar's friends decided to kill him.

In the revised paragraph that follows, the addition of the transitional phrases, "For this reason . . ." and "Even so . . . ," helps a lot.

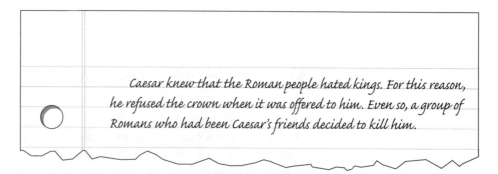

Caesar knew that the Roman people hated kings. For this reason, he refused the crown when it was offered to him. Even so, a group of Romans who had been Caesar's friends decided to kill him.

Common Problem 4: Monotonous Writing

A piece of writing in which the same words are repeated over and over again and every sentence sounds the same will be boring—and "boring" is one thing a writer wants not to be. For example, here is a rather dull paragraph a student wrote about the climate in the region in which she lives:

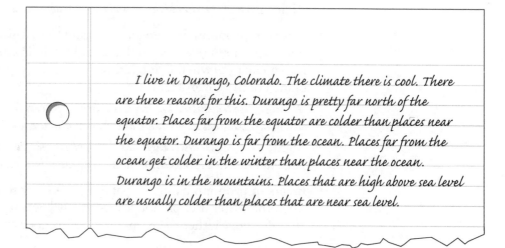

I live in Durango, Colorado. The climate there is cool. There are three reasons for this. Durango is pretty far north of the equator. Places far from the equator are colder than places near the equator. Durango is far from the ocean. Places far from the ocean get colder in the winter than places near the ocean. Durango is in the mountains. Places that are high above sea level are usually colder than places that are near sea level.

19

Notice that the word *Durango* comes up three times in the paragraph, and the word *places* appears six times. Also notice that every single sentence begins with the grammatical subject. In the following example, the writer improved the paragraph by cutting down on repetition and adding **sentence variety**—that is, changing some of the sentences around so they don't all sound alike.

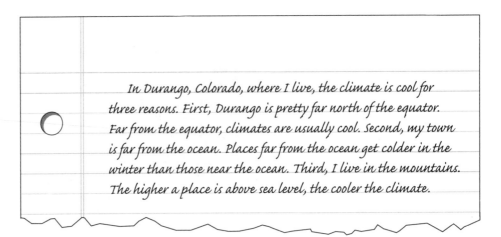

In Durango, Colorado, where I live, the climate is cool for three reasons. First, Durango is pretty far north of the equator. Far from the equator, climates are usually cool. Second, my town is far from the ocean. Places far from the ocean get colder in the winter than those near the ocean. Third, I live in the mountains. The higher a place is above sea level, the cooler the climate.

Common Problem 5: Language Mistakes

Even a clear, lively, well-written paragraph or essay will not pass muster if its sentences are filled with errors in spelling, grammar, and punctuation. Most language arts textbooks include a handbook of grammar, usage, and mechanics that has hundreds of rules. What follows here is a shorthand version of such a handbook. The list of six language errors to avoid is far from comprehensive, but it can work well as a troubleshooter to diagnose and fix many language mistakes in first drafts.

- **Errors in subject-verb agreement.** A verb must always agree with its subject. In the following sentence, the subject is the word *each*, which is singular. Therefore the verb should be singular—as the correction shows.

  Wrong: *Each of the three branches of the U.S. government **are** equally important.*

  Right: *Each of the three branches of the U.S. government **is** equally important.*

- **Errors in pronoun reference.** A writer must always make clear which noun a pronoun refers to. In the first of the following two sentences, the reader can't tell whether *it* refers to the legislative branch or the judicial branch of the government.

  Wrong: *The legislative branch has different powers from the judicial branch. **It** can make decisions about laws, but it cannot make laws.*

  Right: *The legislative branch has different powers from the judicial branch. **The judicial branch** can make decisions about laws, but it cannot make laws.*

- **Errors in pronoun case.** A paragraph or essay sounds sloppy and careless when the writer uses pronouns incorrectly because he or she is not paying attention to whether the pronoun is a subject or an object in the sentence.

I, she, he, we, and *they* are always correct if the pronoun is the subject of a sentence. *Me, her, him, us,* and *them* are always correct if the pronoun is the direct object or indirect object of the verb, or the object of a preposition.

Wrong: *Janet and **me** agree on the issue of gun control.*

Right: *Janet and **I** agree on the issue of gun control.*

I is correct because it is part of the subject of the sentence.

- **Misplaced and dangling modifiers.**   A writer must always make clear which word another word or a phrase is describing. The first of the following two sentences is confusing because it leads the reader to think that the president's staff *is* the chief executive. In the corrected sentence, it is obvious that the phrase *chief executive* refers to the president.

  Wrong: *As **chief executive of our nation,** the president's staff is very large.*

  Right: *The president, as **chief executive of our nation,** needs a very large staff.*

- **Errors in verb forms.**   In most writing for school, students should never use a past participle without a helping verb.

  Wrong: *I **seen** the debates on television.*

  Right: *I **have seen** the debates on television.*

  Also right: *I **saw** the debates on television.*

Writers should always use a past participle—not the simple past—with a helping verb.

  Wrong: *The witness said that the defendant **had stole** the money.*

  Right: *The witness said that the defendant **had stolen** the money.*

Another verb problem is overdependence on the passive voice. Sentences in the active voice sound stronger and livelier.

  Weak: *A bill must **be passed** by both houses of Congress before it can become a law.*

  Better: *Both houses of Congress **must pass** a bill before it can become a law.*

The active voice is almost always preferable to the passive. Reserve the passive voice for only two cases:

1. When the person acted upon is more important than the person(s) doing the acting, as in the following sentence: "One of the candidates **will be elected.**"
2. When the writer doesn't know who or what caused the action, as in the following sentence: "The candidate **was assassinated.**"

- **Missing or misplaced commas.**   The purpose of punctuation is to make writing clear and easy to understand. As in the first of the following two sentences, a comma belongs after introductory phrases or clauses.

  Wrong: *Although the president has the power to veto a bill passed by Congress Congress can override the president's veto.*

  Right: *Although the president has the power to veto a bill passed by Congress, Congress can override the president's veto.*

21

THE FINAL DRAFT OF AN ESSAY

To wrap things up, let's go back to the draft essay about the beliefs and practices of Islam and see how the writer improved it by revising, editing, and proofreading. The changes the student writer made appear in boldface type.

Islam: Beliefs and Practices

Islam, which is one of the great religions of the world, is based on a few important beliefs and expects its believers to follow certain practices. Some of the practices are duties (like rules), and some are customs (traditions that followers do but don't <u>have</u> to do).

*The beliefs of Islam are mostly about God and about Muhammad, who brought the words of God to the Muslim people. Like Christians and Jews, **Muslims** believe in only one God. **Their God, called Allah, is the same God worshiped by Christians and Jews.** Muslims believe that God sent the angel Gabriel to bring God's messages to a man named Muhammad in the 600s. The words God spoke to Muhammad through Gabriel **are** written down in the Muslim holy book, called the Koran.*

*Muslims practice their religion by doing certain duties that they have to do. These duties are called the Five Pillars of Islam. The first is to state "there is only one God" and to agree that Muhammad was his messenger. The second duty is to pray five times a day. Muslims must wash before praying, and at different times during their prayers they must stand, bow, kneel, and lie down. The third duty is to give money to the poor. The fourth is to fast in the daytime during Ramadan. Ramadan is the **ninth** month of the Muslim year. The fifth duty is to travel to Mecca to pray. Mecca is a holy city for Muslims because Muhammad was born there.*

Muslims must not eat pork, and they must not ever drink alcohol. These are rules, too, but they tell people what they must <u>not</u> do instead of what they <u>must</u> do.

Muslims also practice their religion by following certain customs. They don't have to do these things, but most Muslims do them. Examples of Muslim customs are feasting after Ramadan is over and having a big party in honor of a boy or girl who has memorized a large section of the Koran.

Islam is one of the world's newer religions. It started hundreds of years after Christianity and thousands of years after Judaism. Yet, with more than 1 billion followers, it has become one of the great religions of the world.

HANDING IN THE PARAGRAPH OR ESSAY

This is the time to check that a student is giving a teacher a paragraph or an essay in the form that the teacher asked for. Did the teacher announce a preference on any of the following matters?

- Handwriting (pencil or pen) versus typing or word processing?
- Single- or double-spaced?
- Writing on one side or both sides of the paper?
- Position of heading (with name, class, date, anything else requested)?
- Size of margins?

SPECIAL KINDS OF WRITING

In addition to expecting students to write paragraphs and essays like the ones illustrated in the preceding pages, teachers often come up with special kinds of writing assignments. We'll list some of them here and offer a pointer or two about each one.

Editorial/Letter of Persuasion

- Writer must base his or her opinions on facts.
- Writer should acknowledge what critics will say about his or her opinion and show why the writer's opinion actually makes more sense than the critic's.
- Writer should appeal to readers' minds *and* hearts whenever possible.

Personal Narrative or Eyewitness Report

- Writer should make readers feel as if they are experiencing the event themselves. Writer can help accomplish this goal by writing in strict time order—that is, by putting every part of an event in the correct sequence and using expressions such as *at first, then, later, at the same time.*
- Writer should quote what he, she, or someone else said during the event.

Character Sketch

- Writer has to go beyond physical description to communicate the subject's personality.
- Writer should try to convey a dominant, or overall, impression about the character.
- Writer should not just *tell* what the character does but should *show* the character in action.

Business Letters

- Writer has to be especially clear, courteous, complete, and careful (no errors!). This advice applies even in a letter of complaint, when the writer may feel angry.
- Writer should follow a good model that shows where each element of a business letter belongs: heading with date, inside address, salutation, body, closing/signature/typed name.

Comparison/Contrast

- Writer has to decide on a method of organization. One option is to discuss first all the similarities between two items and then all the differences. Another is to discuss both items, feature by feature, and show for each feature whether the two items are alike or different.

Directions; How-to Writing

- Writer must use very clear and precise wording.
- Writer must be careful to keep directions in correct order, never telling the reader to complete any step before another step that must be done first.

Stories, Poems, and Plays

- Writer may model a new story, poem, or play on a published one by an author whom people admire, but the writer must acknowledge this kind of "borrowing." Reading lots of stories, poems, and plays is the best preparation for writing them.
- Writer may create historical fiction by taking a real event from history and imagining what the people said and how they acted during the event.
- Writer may make up a character by combining details from several real people.

! Implications

> To answer the questions, "Why do I have to learn how to write?" and "Why do I have to write so much?," share the following insights with your child.

- **Practice helps.**   One of the most important purposes of writing in school is to help students *become* better writers. Time and again, we see that the very act of writing makes people into better writers.
- **Writing is a way of learning.**   We've all heard that the best way to understand something is to explain it to someone else. And the most challenging way to explain something is in writing rather than face to face.
- **Writing gives people something to show for all their schoolwork.**   For everyone's complaints about having to write in school, many, many adults have a box or a file somewhere that contains the essays they wrote when they were in school. No one seems to keep multiple-choice tests or short-answer homework assignments. People who save their writing can enjoy looking back and saying, "That's pretty good!" or "I remember learning about that."

Skills Practice

> The following activities give your child practice in applying the skills basic to writing paragraphs and essays. For some of the activities, your child may need to review the information in the preceding pages.

A.   JUDGING AN INTRODUCTION TO AN ESSAY

> With your child, read over the following introductions to an essay on the First Amendment to the U.S. Constitution. Ask your child to tell which is the better introduction and to explain why.

- The First Amendment to the Constitution gives four important rights to people in the United States. They are freedom of religion, freedom of speech, freedom of assembly, and freedom of the press.
- The First Amendment to the Constitution gives four important rights to people in the United States. The first is freedom of religion.

Answer

The first introduction is better than the second. Both introductions begin with a good opening sentence, or thesis statement. However, the first one gives a complete overview of the essay, which will have one paragraph on each of the four freedoms. The second introduction names only one of the four freedoms that the essay will discuss.

B. JUDGING A TOPIC SENTENCE FOR A PARAGRAPH

With your child, read over the following sentences for a paragraph about freedom of speech as described in the First Amendment to the Constitution. Ask your child to tell which is the better topic sentence and to explain why.

- Freedom of speech means that the government cannot punish people for expressing their ideas, no matter what their ideas may be.
- According to the First Amendment, speech includes actions, such as marching or holding a demonstration, even if people are not saying anything.

Answer

The first sentence is better than the second sentence as a topic sentence for a paragraph about freedom of speech. The first sentence gives an overview of the whole paragraph. The second example sentence gives a detail about freedom of speech rather than an overview of the topic.

C. JUDGING SUPPORTING SENTENCES

With your child, read over these sentences to follow the first of the preceding topic sentences in a paragraph about the freedom of speech. Ask your child to tell which is the better supporting sentence and to explain why.

- The government can punish people for crimes such as robbery and murder.
- Even though we have freedom of speech, telling lies that could hurt another person is against the law.

Answer

For the stated purpose, the second example sentence is better than the first example sentence. The second sentence gives a detail related to the general idea expressed by the topic sentence in Practice B, whereas the first sentence is off the topic of the topic sentence in Practice B.

D. JUDGING A CONCLUSION TO AN ESSAY

With your child, read over the following conclusions to an essay on the First Amendment to the U.S. Constitution. Ask your child to tell which is the better conclusion and to explain why.

- The other nine amendments that make up the Bill of Rights give people in the United States important freedoms. But without the four freedoms named in the First Amendment, a true democracy would be impossible.
- The First Amendment to the U.S. Constitution is part of the Bill of Rights. The Bill of Rights contains the first ten amendments to the constitution.

Answer

The first sample conclusion is better because it summarizes the essay by mentioning the four freedoms in the First Amendment and adds an idea about how important that amendment is. The second sample conclusion introduces a new idea—that the first ten amendments to the Constitution are called the Bill of Rights—but it doesn't sum up information about the First Amendment, nor does it add ideas that are relevant to the First Amendment.

Evaluating Your Child's Skills (Practices A, B, C, and D): In order to complete these activities successfully, your child will need to apply what he or she has learned to samples from paragraphs and essays, compare and contrast those samples, make judgments, and give reasons for those judgments. If your child needs help making valid judgments, reread with him or her the appropriate advice from the section called "What Your Child Needs to Know," and explain how the better models follow that advice.

E. REVISING, EDITING, AND PROOFREADING A PARAGRAPH

Here again is the first draft of the student paragraph about the three branches of the U.S. government. Encourage your child to read it over, thinking about how it could be improved, and then to revise it. You might wish to "conference" with your child about the paragraph first.

The U.S. government is divided into three branches—the executive, the legislative, and the judicial. The executive branch include the president, the vice president, the president's cabinet, the Executive Office of the President, and many federal agencies. Examples of federal agencies are the Environmental Protection Agency and the U.S. Post Office. There are many federal agencies. The purpose of the executive branch is to enforce the laws of our country. The legislative branch is made up of the Senate and the House of Representatives, which are the two houses of Congress. This branches' purpose is to make laws for our country. It's important for every country to have laws. The judicial branch is made up of federal judges. These judges make decisions about whether laws are constitutional. They are apointed by the president. They also preside over trials for federal crimes.

The U.S. government is divided into three branches—the executive, the legislative, and the judicial. The executive branch **includes** the president, the vice president, the president's cabinet, the Executive Office of the President, and many federal agencies. Examples of federal agencies are the Environmental Protection Agency and the U.S. Post Office. **‹sentence deleted›** The purpose of the executive branch is to enforce the laws of our country. The legislative branch is made up of the Senate and the House of Representatives, which are the two houses of Congress. This **branch's** purpose is to make laws for our country. **‹sentence deleted›** The judicial branch is made up of federal judges. They are **appointed** by the president. These judges make decisions about whether laws are constitutional. They also preside over trials for federal crimes.

Suggested Answers

Note the three corrections in boldface type and the deletion of two sentences.

> ***Evaluating Your Child's Skills:*** In order to complete this activity successfully, your child will need to use his or her judgment in deciding what needs to be changed in the sample paragraph. Your child will also need to apply what he or she has learned from this book and perhaps in language arts classes about organizing a paragraph, constructing sentences, and using language correctly. See the section of this chapter called "Troubleshooting: Improving the Piece of Writing and Removing Errors" for guidance if your child has trouble.

Top of the Class

> If your child has mastered the basics of writing a solid paragraph and a well-organized essay, he or she may appreciate some pointers on how to add one or more features that will make his or her writing really stand out.

WRITE AN OUTSTANDING INTRODUCTION

> While a clearly written introduction that gives a general overview of an essay is perfectly satisfactory, an introduction that grabs the reader's attention is even better.

If you're writing an essay, try writing an introductory paragraph that will get readers (and that probably includes your teacher) to take notice. For example, an essay about the First Amendment to the Constitution could start like this:

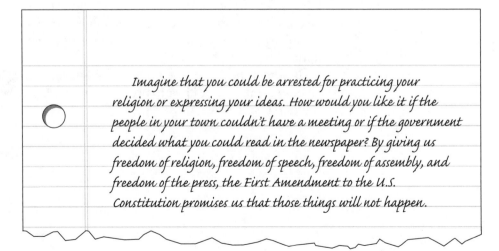

Imagine that you could be arrested for practicing your religion or expressing your ideas. How would you like it if the people in your town couldn't have a meeting or if the government decided what you could read in the newspaper? By giving us freedom of religion, freedom of speech, freedom of assembly, and freedom of the press, the First Amendment to the U.S. Constitution promises us that those things will not happen.

INCLUDE ADDITIONAL INFORMATION

> **While the paragraphs and essays we've been discussing are not research papers but are based on information students have already learned about, a little research for an essay that is written at home can show that your child is seriously considering the topic.**

Suppose you are writing an essay about Islam, like the one given as an example early in this chapter. The essay will be fine if you include the important information you learned about Islam from your textbook and class discussions. It will be even better if you include some interesting information that you found on your own. For example, if you look up *Islam* in an encyclopedia, you might find out that the journey Muslims must take to Mecca is called a pilgrimage, or a *hajj*. You might also learn that when Muslims reach Mecca they must walk seven times around a building called the Kaaba and kiss the sacred black stone in its wall.

Additional details like these can make your essay more interesting and show your teacher that you took the trouble to find out more about your topic than what you read in your textbook. Be sure to tell where you got your information. See Chapter 3, on research, to find out how to list your sources correctly.

USE VIVID LANGUAGE

> **In addition to correcting mistakes when revising a paragraph or an essay, your child can improve his or her piece of writing even more by changing a few ordinary words to ones that are more vivid, precise, or descriptive.**

In general, when writing a paragraph or an essay for a school assignment, it's best to stick with clear, simple language and not try to get too fancy. However, you can make your writing stand out by changing just one or two ordinary words to ones that get your meaning across even better. For example, in the paragraph about Islam, you could change "The beliefs of Islam are **mostly** about God . . ." to "The beliefs of Islam are **primarily** about God. . . ." Or you could change "Muslims practice their religion by **doing** certain duties **that they have to do**" to "Muslims practice their religion by **performing** certain **compulsory** duties."

If you want to spruce up your language, a thesaurus can be a big help. Choose some plain old words you've used and find better synonyms for them. But don't get carried away.

CHAPTER 2

Book Reports

What Your Child Needs to Know

> You may choose to use the following text in several different ways, depending on your child's strengths and preferences. You might read the passage aloud; you might read it to yourself and then paraphrase it for your child; or you might ask your child to read the material along with you or on his or her own.

To determine how well students are learning to read, to express themselves, and to work independently, the language arts curriculum has long called for written **book reports.** Nowadays, though, book reports aren't limited to language arts. Teachers also ask students to write reports on books related to social studies and science. So while the class studies, say, natural habitats as part of geography or earth science, don't be surprised to find that students have to read and report on a related fiction title such as *Sarah, Plain and Tall* by Patricia MacLachlan (HarperCollins, 1985) or a related nonfiction title such as *A City Under the Sea: Life in a Coral Reef* by Norbert Wu (Simon & Schuster, 1996).

Some teachers give their students detailed directions on how to move through the book report process, from selecting a book to submitting a written report. Other teachers may leave the assignment more open-ended, expecting students to figure out on their own what to do and when to do it. This chapter offers advice for either situation. It covers the following topics: choosing a book for a book report, scheduling the work, taking notes while reading, organizing a book report, writing a first draft, self-evaluating and revising a book report, and considering alternatives to standard book reports.

CHOOSING A BOOK FOR A BOOK REPORT

Perhaps the teacher, working with the school librarian, has selected and set aside for the students copies of several different books. The teacher may have given the students a list describing each of the books. In that case, it should be relatively easy to select a book from the group.

On the other hand, the teacher may suggest a kind of book or a particular topic for a book report but may expect each child to find an appropriate book on his or her own. In this case, the teacher may also have told the students to bring in for approval the books they have chosen. In this situation or if the teacher has said only, "Write a book report on a book about what we are covering in class," here are suggestions to help choose a book.

1. A student's textbook may list other books about each chapter. Look at the end of a chapter or the end of the textbook for a list called something like "For Further Reading" or "A Bibliography for Students."
2. The student can go with a friend or an adult to the local public library. There, in the children's room, the student can look up the assigned topic in the **catalog** or can ask the **librarian** to point out the shelves with books on the topic. The student should then examine the books and ask the librarian other questions, if necessary.

3. The student can use a home or school computer and the Internet to search the library catalog for books by author, title, or subject. The computer will even indicate if the book is available or when it will be back in the library.
4. The student or parent can check *Best Books for Children* by John T. Gillespie (R. R. Bowker, 2001). This is a large reference book that identifies titles appropriate for students at each grade level. It is available in most public libraries.
5. To figure out if a library book is appropriate, a student can try the Five-Finger Test, which is used at the Copper Hill Elementary School in Raritan Township, New Jersey.

Five-Finger Test

a. Open the book near its middle.
b. Hold up five fingers, and begin to read the page.
c. Put down a finger for each word you do not know.
d. If you put down all five fingers, the book may be too hard for you now.
e. If you finish the page and are still holding up one or more fingers, this book may be for you.

SCHEDULING THE WORK

For the record, after choosing a book and getting it approved, if necessary, the usual stages for a book report project include the following:

- Reading a certain number of pages or chapters a day
- Thinking about the book and taking notes while reading it
- Organizing the book report
- Writing a first draft
- Improving the first draft of the book report and handing it in

(The teacher may, of course, modify one or more of the stages.)

Here are a few general questions a reader should consider when reading a work of **fiction** or a work of **nonfiction.** Answers to the questions will indicate whether the process of reading is getting off to a good start.

Questions to Ask for a Work of Fiction

- How does the novel begin?
- Which characters have I met so far?
- What do I like and not like about each character? Would I want to be friends with him or her? Why?
- Is the story making me feel happy or sad? How come?
- Is the story going along the way I expected it to, or has something unexpected happened? If so, what?

Questions to Ask for a Work of Nonfiction

- Am I enjoying the book? Why or why not?
- How do the words and the illustrations, if any, work together?
- What have I learned from the book that I didn't know before?
- How would I judge the way the author writes? Is he or she clear? Does he or she give enough examples? Is the writing lively or boring?

THINKING AND TAKING NOTES WHILE READING

Without writing anything down, some readers can keep track of what they read and the ideas that come to them while reading. Other readers might benefit from a suggestion that they write themselves notes about the book as they read or immediately after each reading session. The notes do not have to be formal. They just have to remind a reader of events, places, and characters in the book. The reader can put the notes in his or her own words or might choose to copy a passage out of the book and then tell what he or she thinks about that passage. The notes can go in a paper journal, in a computer file, or on note cards that the reader keeps in the book. The bottom line is that the notes can help immensely when it comes time for the reader to prepare the book report itself.

Here are examples of reminder notes (and page numbers) that a reader might jot down for the historical novel *The Courage of Sarah Noble* by Alice Dalgliesh (Macmillan, 1954).

page 6: Sarah is kind—she worries about Thomas, the horse.

page 18: Sarah's father is a good man—he has respect for all people, including the Indians.

p. 36: Father says, "To be afraid and to be brave is the best courage of all." This means it takes more courage to be brave when you're scared than when you're not.

p. 49: Tall John calls Sarah "daughter."

Here are examples of reminder notes (and page numbers) that a reader might jot down for the nonfiction title *What's the Big Idea, Ben Franklin?* by Jean Fritz (Putnam, 1996).

---

p. 3—Poor Richard's Almanac

p. 10—experiment with electricity (kite and key)

p. 13—postal system

p. 20—helped write the Declaration of Independence

p. 27—helped write the Constitution

ORGANIZING A BOOK REPORT

Some teachers will give oral or written directions on what book reports should look like and say. These teachers may tell students how many words to write. They may even give students a **template,** or form, with questions or headings and room to write in answers or ideas. If the teacher has not given such directions, here are two options for a standard book report (and at the end of this chapter we give alternatives to the standard book report).

Setting Up a Book Report as a Form

One option is to write a book report that is set up as a form—with headings. Here are examples of a form for a novel and a form for a nonfiction book. (See forms on following pages.)

Student name   Date

Class

REPORT ON A NOVEL

OPENING

Title:

Author:

BODY

Names of Main Characters and Descriptions:

Setting:

Summary of Story:

CONCLUSION

Opinion, Recommendation, and Reasons:

Sample form for a novel

Student name   Date

Class

REPORT ON A NONFICTION BOOK
OPENING

   Title:

   Author:

BODY

   Kind of Book:

   Main Idea:

   Details That Support or Illustrate the Main Idea:

CONCLUSION

   Opinion, Recommendation, and Reasons:

Sample form for a nonfiction book

A finished model of a book report set up as a form appears later in this chapter.

Setting Up a Book Report as a Regular Composition

Another option is to produce a book report in the form of a regular composition or essay. This kind of book report will not have headings written out, but keeping them in mind helps the writer to organize the composition. See the complete model later in this chapter.

WRITING A FIRST DRAFT

Opening

The basic opening for a book report immediately identifies the book by title, author, and kind of book. Following are models of basic openings for book reports. Models A and B are for a fiction book—one set up as a form and one set up as a regular composition. Models C and D are for a nonfiction book—one set up as a form and one set up as a regular composition.

Model A

> **Title:** <u>The Courage of Sarah Noble</u>
> **Author:** Alice Dalgliesh
> **Kind of Book:** Historical novel published in 1954. This book is based on a true story about a girl who left Massachusetts in 1707 to help her father while he built the first house in New Milford, Connecticut.

Model B

> <u>The Courage of Sarah Noble</u> by Alice Dalgliesh is a historical novel published in 1954. It is based on a true story.

Model C

Title: *What's the Big Idea, Ben Franklin?*
Author: Jean Fritz
Kind of Book: Biography of Benjamin Franklin published in 1976

Model D

What's the Big Idea, Ben Franklin? by Jean Fritz is a biography of Benjamin Franklin published in 1976. It doesn't tell about Franklin's whole life but concentrates on his most important ideas and accomplishments.

Attention-Getting Openers

Sometimes an opening can be more of an attention-getter, as in the following two examples. While the basic opening begins with information about the author, title, and kind of book, in the attention-getter, the writer tries to grab the reader's interest before providing basic information about the book.

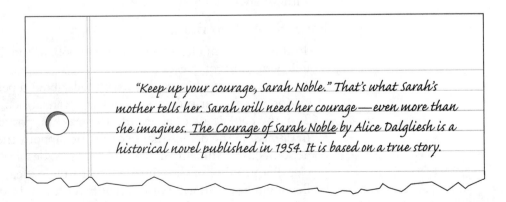

"Keep up your courage, Sarah Noble." That's what Sarah's mother tells her. Sarah will need her courage—even more than she imagines. *The Courage of Sarah Noble* by Alice Dalgliesh is a historical novel published in 1954. It is based on a true story.

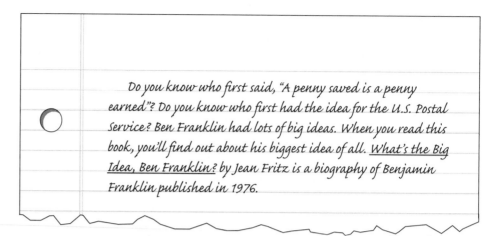

Do you know who first said, "A penny saved is a penny earned"? Do you know who first had the idea for the U.S. Postal Service? Ben Franklin had lots of big ideas. When you read this book, you'll find out about his biggest idea of all. <u>What's the Big Idea, Ben Franklin?</u> by Jean Fritz is a biography of Benjamin Franklin published in 1976.

Body

When a reader fills in the next sections of the form or drafts the body of a composition about a book, he or she has to think about the book as a whole, as well as its details. Here are some pointers.

For a Novel

- To describe the **characters** of a novel, a student can tell what they look like, how they act, how they speak and think, and what other people in the book say about them. A student can also mention whether the characters are believable and whether the author makes readers care about the characters. Whenever possible, the student should provide one or two examples to back up general statements about a character.
- To describe the **setting** of a novel, a student must tell when and where the novel takes place. Sometimes it is helpful for the student not only to give the dates but to identify the historical period more directly—for example, "The novel takes place in New England in the 1770s, during the American Revolution."
- To provide an effective **summary of the plot** of a novel, the student should report what happens in chronological, or time, order. The summary should be more than just a list of unrelated incidents in the book. It should give the reader of the report a clear sense of the main action of the book—without giving away the ending.

For a Nonfiction Book

- To state the main idea of a nonfiction book, a student should consider the following kinds of questions:
  1. If the book is a **biography,** which tells about a person, what were (or are) the person's most important traits, or characteristics?
  2. If the book is about an event, why was it important to people?
- In discussing the details that back up, or support, the main idea of a nonfiction book, a student should provide facts, descriptive details, or examples. For instance, if the student says the main idea of a book is that Benjamin Franklin was both a great inventor and a great statesman, the

student must give examples of Franklin's inventions and mention his contributions to the American Revolution and to the Constitution.

Conclusion

Whether or not a student hints at his or her opinion about the book in the opening of the report, the end of the report must make clear the student's thoughts and feelings about the reading experience. The student should include a generalization—did he or she like the book or not?—and details or reasons to support the generalization. In addition, the student should mention other people who might benefit from reading the book. Here are sample questions the student might ask himself or herself in order to form a judgment about the book.

For a Novel

- Is the novel—even if it is science fiction or fantasy—believable? Why?
- What did the novel teach me about other people or about myself?
- What particular parts of the novel do I remember most? What makes me remember these parts?
- What kinds of people would find this novel enjoyable or helpful?
- Would I read another novel by this author? Why?
- How does this novel compare with other novels I have read?

For a Nonfiction Book

- Is the topic of the book important to me? Why?
- Is the book lively and interesting or dull and dry?
- What particular parts of the book do I remember most? What makes me remember these parts?
- What kinds of people would find this book enjoyable or helpful?
- Would I read another book on this topic or another book by this author? Why?

Quoting from a Book

Usually, a teacher wants to read the student's own words about a book—not a series of lines quoted directly from the book. However, using a phrase or sentence from the book can be effective. Here are examples of working in a quotation.

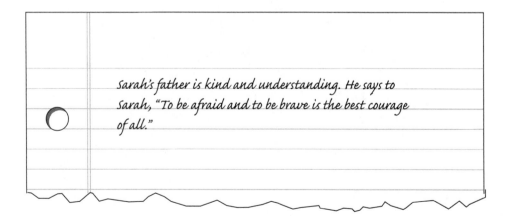

Sarah's father is kind and understanding. He says to Sarah, "To be afraid and to be brave is the best courage of all."

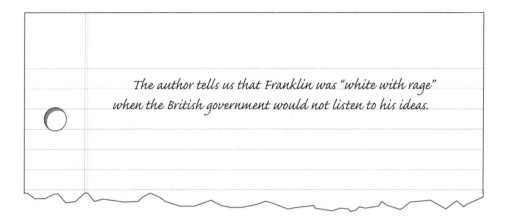

The author tells us that Franklin was "white with rage" when the British government would not listen to his ideas.

Making Up a Title for a Book Report

If a book report is set up as a form, the following titles are appropriate:

A Book Report about a Novel

A Report about a Nonfiction Book

If a book report is written as a regular composition, the teacher may give advice about making up a title. If the teacher has not given any direction, here are examples of titles for a book report. The examples are for a report about *The Courage of Sarah Noble*.

A Book Report on *The Courage of Sarah Noble*

My Thoughts about *The Courage of Sarah Noble*

The Courage of Sarah Noble and Colonial Times

MODELS OF BOOK REPORTS

Model A presented here shows a book report set up as a form with headings. Model B shows a book report as a regular composition without headings. Both models have an opening, a body, and a conclusion.

Model A

Opening

Title: What's the Big Idea, Ben Franklin?
Author: Jean Fritz
Kind of Book: This is a biography of Benjamin Franklin published in 1976. It doesn't give all the facts about Franklin's whole life, but it tells about his biggest ideas and the most important things he did.

Main Idea: The main idea of this book is that Benjamin Franklin was a man who had many important ideas. He was a writer and an inventor. His ideas also helped the American colonies become the United States of America.

Body

Support for Main Idea (or *Important Details*): In this biography, the author tells that Franklin published a book called Poor Richard's Almanac. This book is full of many famous sayings we still use today, such as "A penny saved is a penny earned." We also learn that Franklin did important experiments with electricity and invented the lightning rod. The U.S. Postal Service was Franklin's idea! Benjamin Franklin was also very important because he helped to write both the Declaration of Independence and the Constitution.

Conclusion

Opinion, Recommendation, and Reasons: I liked reading this book because the author writes in a lively way and isn't always serious. She tells some funny stories about Franklin. For example, she tells how he used to eat too much and call himself "Dr. Fatsides." Even though Benjamin Franklin was a great man, the author makes him seem like a regular person. I recommend What's the Big Idea, Ben Franklin? to anyone who wants to read a book that tells about American history and is funny at the same time.

Model B

A Book Report on <u>The Courage of Sarah Noble</u>

Opening

"Keep up your courage, Sarah Noble." That's what Sarah's mother tells her. Sarah will need her courage—even more than she imagines. <u>The Courage of Sarah Noble</u> by Alice Dalgliesh is a historical novel published in 1954. It is based on a true story.

The main characters are Sarah and her father. Sarah is a very brave eight-year-old girl. She has to face many dangers, but she keeps her courage. Sarah's father is kind and understanding. He says to Sarah, "To be afraid and to be brave is the best courage of all."

Body

The story takes place in 1707. Sarah and her father are leaving Massachusetts for Connecticut, where Sarah's father is going to build a house. The area around New Milford is wilderness, and only Indians live there.

Sarah has to go with her father because he needs someone to cook for him, and Sarah's mother has to stay home with the baby. When they get to the place where the house will be, they live in a hut. An Indian they call "Tall John" helps Sarah's father build the house, and Sarah makes friends with Tall John's children. Then Sarah's father goes back for the rest of the family. Sarah stays with Tall John's family. She worries about unfriendly Indians who might attack them, and she worries that something will happen to her family. But she never loses her courage.

Conclusion

I enjoyed <u>The Courage of Sarah Noble</u> because I admired Sarah for being so brave. The only thing I'd like to know is why Sarah's father couldn't cook for himself or take one of his older sons to help him. I would recommend this book to anyone who likes reading about colonial times and anyone who likes reading stories of courage.

SELF-EVALUATING AND REVISING A BOOK REPORT

After the first draft, it is a good idea to put a book report away for a day or so and then come back to it with fresh eyes. Here is a list of questions a student can ask while reading the draft. Most writers make changes in their first drafts at this point. They may add information, drop sentences, and rearrange parts of the report.

Checklist for Evaluating and Revising a Book Report

1. Did I remember to identify the book and its author?
2. Did I make clear what kind of book it is (for example, a historical novel, a biography)?
3. If the book is a novel, did I tell enough about the characters, the setting, and the plot?
4. If the book is nonfiction, did I tell enough about its main idea and the details that support or illustrate that idea?
5. Did I make my opinion about the book clear, and did I give enough reasons for my opinion?
6. Did I identify other people who I think should read the book?
7. Did I remember to underline or use italics every time I mentioned the title of the book?
8. Did I check my report for grammar, usage, spelling, capitalization, and punctuation?

CONSIDERING ALTERNATIVES TO STANDARD BOOK REPORTS

Some teachers are open to alternatives to the standard types of reports, illustrated previously. A student may ask if one of the following alternatives would be acceptable.

- **Oral book report.** In this kind of report, a student gives the report orally, working from an outline or note cards. This project requires speaking clearly, making eye contact with the audience, and preparing and using visuals. It also requires rehearsal.
- **Sales talk.** A variation on the preceding idea involves taking on the role of a sales representative from the company that published the book. The student can pretend he or she is talking to the owner of a bookstore and trying to persuade the owner to buy several copies of the book.
- **Letter to the author.** This kind of report should not describe characters, summarize a plot, or explain the main idea of the book. Instead, it should evaluate the book, telling what if anything was confusing and asking questions about the author and the process of writing the book.
- **A mock interview with a character or real person from the book.** A student can write up or perform an interview in which he or she plays both the interviewer and the interviewee. The student can make up five or ten questions to ask a character in a novel or the subject of a biography and can provide possible answers.

- **A diary entry by a character in a novel or the subject of a biography.** A student may get into a character's or a real person's mind and write a diary or journal entry that the character or person might have written—either in response to an incident in the book or to an incident that takes place outside the boundaries of the book.
- **Dramatization of a scene from the book.** Working with classmates, a student may be able to create a script involving a character or real person from the book, as well as other characters or real people. The group will first have to convert the narration in the book into a script and then will have to rehearse and perform in front of the rest of the class or perhaps on a videotape for the whole class to watch and evaluate.

! Implications

> Discussing the following ideas may help motivate your child by encouraging him or her to think of a book report as more than just a chore.

- A student may think of a book report as just another job he or she has to do because the teacher gave the assignment. But a student could think of a book report as a chance to express his or her opinion about something and try to persuade others to share the opinion.
- A student's book report may help other young people make decisions about which books to read. If friends and classmates later choose to read a book a student has reported on, they all will have something in common—something new and interesting to talk about.
- A student can keep book reports on file and someday make them available to younger kids—kids who are the age the student is now. The student's reports might help those children of the future to choose books they enjoy reading. The teacher might keep book reports on file for future classes to read.
- Did the student ever notice that most major newspapers and many magazines have **book review** sections? Some people make book reviewing and reporting on books their career. This fact should tell the student that many people are interested in reading book reviews. Many people consider reading books to be an important part of their lives, and book reviews help them decide what they want to read.

 # Skills Practice

> Your child may still need help with the process discussed in the section called "What Your Child Needs to Know." Or perhaps your child has made an attempt at a book report and now needs to clarify

a few points in order to revise his or her first draft. The following activities are provided for children who need additional help, reinforcement, or practice. The models used in each activity are based on *Little House on the Prairie* (HarperCollins, 1935), the third book in the beloved series of historical novels by Laura Ingalls Wilder.

A. WRITING AN OPENING FOR A BOOK REPORT

With your child, read over the following openings for a book report. Ask your child to tell which is the better opening and to explain why.

1. Which is the better, more complete opening for a basic book report?
   * *Little House on the Prairie* by Laura Ingalls Wilder is a historical novel published in 1935. It is fiction, but it is based on real events from the author's childhood.
   * The book I read is about people who went to live on the prairie. The book was published a long time ago.
2. Of the two following openers, which gets your attention?
   * The Ingalls family leaves Wisconsin and heads for the land west of the Mississippi. This book tells what happens to them.
   * The Ingalls family leaves their cozy house in Wisconsin and heads out for the wild land west of the Mississippi. Do they know what is in store for them? Are they making a mistake?

Answers

1. *The first opener is better because it gives all the necessary information about the book. The second opener leaves out the title, the author's name, and the type of book, and it is vague about its publication date.*
2. *The second opener is a better attention-getter because it makes the reader curious about the book. The first opener doesn't create curiosity or suspense.*

B. DESCRIBING CHARACTERS IN A BOOK REPORT

With your child, read over the following character descriptions. Ask your child to tell which is the better description and to explain why.

* Ma is a loving mother. Even in the wilderness, she makes sure her children have a comfortable home and a good education.
* Ma is a good mother, but she can be bossy. She does good things for her children, but she acts like she always knows best.

Answer

The first character description is better because it supports, or backs up, the first statement with examples. The first statement in the second character description is vague (good is a vague word), and the details that follow are not specific enough to back it up.

C. WRITING A SUMMARY

With your child, read over the following plot summaries. Ask your child to tell which one is best and to explain why.

• Pa thinks the Wisconsin woods are getting too crowded, so he sells their house and builds a covered wagon. The family travels from Wisconsin to Oklahoma, where Pa builds the little house on the prairie. With Ma and Pa, Laura and Mary work hard and face many dangers, including a raging prairie fire that threatens to burn down their house. The way the book ends will make you want to read the next book in the series.

• Pa builds a little house on the prairie in Oklahoma. This happens after he sells their house in Wisconsin and builds a covered wagon to move the family. The whole family works hard on the new house, but then they have to move after living in it for only one year.

• Pa thinks the Wisconsin woods are getting too crowded, so he sells their house and builds a covered wagon. The family travels from Wisconsin to Oklahoma, where Pa builds the little house on the prairie. One time, Pa has to save a neighbor named Mr. Scott from being trapped in a well. Another time, the whole family gets sick and almost dies. At Christmas, another neighbor named Mr. Edwards risks his life to get presents for the children. And once, the family's dog almost gets killed.

Answer

The first summary is the best because it is in correct time order, it gives enough detail to interest the reader but not too much, and it does not give away the ending of the book. The second summary is out of time order, does not give enough detail, and gives away the ending. The third summary gives too many details without saying what they add up to or mean.

D. WRITING A CONCLUSION FOR A BOOK REPORT

With your child, read over the following conclusions. Ask your child to tell which one is better and to explain why.

• I enjoyed reading *Little House on the Prairie* because of the exciting parts of the plot, such as when howling wolves surround the house or when the house almost burns down. But I got bored by the long parts about how the house gets built. I would recommend the book to people who like to read about pioneers—especially if they are interested in how people built houses in those days.

• I liked *Little House on the Prairie*. It was a good book. It had lots of exciting parts and only a few boring parts. I like reading exciting books. I can't wait to read the next book in the series about Laura and her family. I think everyone would enjoy reading this book.

Answer

The first conclusion is better because the writer has backed up general statements with examples. The writer has also recommended the book to a specific audience. The second conclusion makes general statements without backing them up, and the recommendation at the end is too general.

> **Evaluating Your Child's Skills (Practices A, B, C, and D):** In order to complete these activities successfully, your child will need to apply what he or she has learned to models from book reports, compare and contrast those models, make judgments, and give reasons for those judgments. If your child needs help making valid judgments, reread with him or her the appropriate advice from the section called "What Your Child Needs to Know," and explain how the better models follow that advice.

 # Top of the Class

> If your child has mastered the basics of writing a solid book report, he or she may appreciate some pointers on how to add one or more features that will make his or her report really stand out. Here are a few suggestions.

QUOTE PROFESSIONAL REVIEWS

> Let your child know that there are several sites on the Internet that provide professional reviews of children's books. Suggest accessing one or more of these sites to search for the book on which your child is reporting. The search may turn up a review from which your child can quote in order to support or enhance the character descriptions, summary, or conclusion of the report. The source and the reviewer, of course, should be credited. Emphasize that the purpose of the quote is to *support* your child's personal opinion of the book, not to replace it. Here are some examples of sites to visit.

- www.geocities.com/rebeccampahle for Reba's Reading Rampage
- www.mamalisa.com/books for Children's Book Recommendations by Mama Lisa
- www.bookhive.org/bookhive.htm for the Web site of the Public Library of Charlotte and Mecklenburg County, North Carolina
- www.childrenslit.com/th.htm for a subscription-based children's book review service

In addition, the commercial sites amazon.com and barnesandnoble.com provide reviews of children's books by both professionals and readers. (The professional reviews will probably be more useful than the readers' reviews.) And, of course, sometimes quotable reviews can be found right on the back of a book.

INCLUDE INFORMATION ABOUT THE AUTHOR

> **Suggest that a brief paragraph about the author's life, especially if it relates to the book in some way, can be a good ending for a book report.**

Often, such information can be found on the back of a book or on the book jacket. A series called *Something about the Author,* available in the children's rooms of most libraries, provides excellent author biographies. On the Internet, the Children's Book Council's site www.cbcbooks.org provides biographies of authors. Simply using a search engine and typing in the author's name as the key word is another good way to find information about an author.

COMPARE WITH ANOTHER BOOK

> **Suggest to your child that, in the conclusion of a book report, the writer of the report can sometimes really drive a point home by comparing the book to another similar book he or she has read. For example, a report on *Little House on the Prairie* could end with a comparison with *The Courage of Sarah Noble.***

I enjoyed reading *Little House on the Prairie* because of the exciting parts of the plot, such as when howling wolves surround the house or when the house almost burns down. But I got bored by the long parts about how the house gets built. For this reason, I did not enjoy *Little House on the Prairie* as much as another historical novel I read, *The Courage of Sarah Noble,* because in *The Courage of Sarah Noble,* there is not one boring moment.

CHAPTER 3

Research Reports

What Your Child Needs to Know

You may choose to use the following text in several different ways, depending on your child's strengths and preferences. You might read the passage aloud; you might read it to yourself and then paraphrase it for your child; or you might ask your child to read the material along with you or on his or her own.

How does a **research report** (or research "paper") differ from a regular composition or essay and from a book report? The main difference is that in an essay or a book report the student usually depends only on the facts and opinions in his or her head, but in a research report the student usually works with facts and opinions that other people have gathered about a topic or subject. The student finds the facts and opinions in reference works such as **encyclopedias,** in other nonfiction books, on Web sites, and through interviews and personal observation. We use the word *sources* to label these things and people we go to for information. Then the student has to figure out which facts and opinions to use, which to throw out, and how to arrange the facts and opinions he or she has selected. The student must also tell the reader where the facts and ideas come from; that is, the student must identify his or her sources. In addition, some teachers want students to add their own thoughts and opinions to what they have found through research.

Why do schools require students to produce research reports? First and foremost, schools want to teach students to ask questions about the world around them. Then schools want to give students experience in finding answers to their questions. It's been said that knowing the answers is not nearly as important as knowing how and where to find answers. Students who practice asking their own questions and answering them in elementary school and secondary school will be ready to ask serious questions and research the answers outside of school—in the "real world"—while they are still children and when they grow up.

Because teachers expect so much when they assign a research report, students have to understand that to get a good result they have to put in more time than for most other assignments. A research report is not the sort of thing a student can whip up in one sitting. Usually, a research report takes days or even weeks to complete. Sometimes, though, a student leaves too much of the work until the last minute. As a teacher once suggested on a Discovery Channel Web site, kids aren't born with a sense of time management. If they know a research report is due in March, they usually don't worry about it in February. But they really should work on stages of the report in February if they want to avoid panic in March.

Stages is the most important word in the preceding sentence. This chapter will lay out the eight stages that people go through to produce a research report. Each stage should have its own deadline or due date. Often, a teacher will give students a due date for each stage, but if this isn't the case, the student should impose his or her own deadline—perhaps with the guidance of a parent.

STAGE 1: GETTING A TOPIC

There are at least three kinds of teachers when it comes to research reports, and we'll look at an example of each. Let's call them Ms. Alonso, Mr. Becker, and Ms. Chin.

Ms. Alonso gave her students a broad topic, as well as suggestions for narrowing the topic to a more manageable size. The broad topic was *explorers*, and the suggestions included names of daring men and women who lived between the years 1400 and 2000. Ms. Alonso expected each student to pick an explorer, do research about him or her, and write a report answering specific questions listed in the assignment. For example, Ms. Alonso asked, "What made the person you've picked become an explorer?" and "What was your explorer's most famous discovery?"

Mr. Becker gave his students a broad topic but expected them to choose their own subtopics for the research and the report. Specifically, Mr. Becker said, "Your assignment is to write a research report on the ancient Maya culture. Cover three of the following subtopics: history, location, economics, politics, social structure, contributions (science, art, math, and so on)."

Ms. Chin was the kind of teacher who gave even less direction. She said, "Do a research report about any topic you are interested in as long as it has some connection with what we have studied in class." Because the class had been studying immigration to the United States and had looked at old photographs of immigrants getting off ships, one student, Donna Diaz, decided to do a research report about immigrants who entered the United States through Ellis Island.

"I" or No "I"?

When a teacher gives the assignment for a research project, he or she may also announce whether or not students should use the word *I* in their reports. Some teachers want students to avoid using *I*; other teachers want students not only to use *I* but also to talk about themselves throughout the report. See the box about the **I-Search report,** which is growing in popularity.

A Special Kind of Research Report: The I-Search Report

Teachers expect students to say a great deal about themselves in an I-Search report. In such reports, students explain why they are interested in certain topics, how they go about the research, and what they learn about the topic and about themselves in the process. For example, Danny White, another student of Ms. Chin's, wondered: "Can I find out about my great-great-grandfather, Ben Corner, who immigrated to the United States from Romania in the early twentieth century? Did he come through Ellis Island? Where did he sail from? Can I find out where he lived in Romania?" Danny decided to try to answer these questions by doing an I-Search report. We'll check on Danny's progress later in this chapter.

STAGE 2: FINDING AND EVALUATING RESEARCH SOURCES

Sometimes, parents find a number of sources for their children to look over and decide whether to use or not. Sometimes, children hunt for sources on their own. Let's see what sources Donna Diaz, who worked by herself, found about Ellis Island; let's also look at some questions she thought of as she began her research.

Getting an Overview and Generating Research Questions

Donna began by looking up "Ellis Island" in the *World Book* encyclopedia, one of several good general encyclopedias that are useful to students of Donna's age. She could have used the printed encyclopedia in her school or local library, but she preferred to get the latest version of the electronic encyclopedia on the Internet. The *World Book* article on Ellis Island gave Donna some information about the role of the island in immigration. In addition, the article made Donna think of questions, which you can see in the list that follows.

Such questions, called **research questions,** are very important. They "kick off" the report by helping the student focus on what information he or she wants to include in the report and by steering the student toward additional sources. Some teachers give students a list of research questions. Otherwise, students need to come up with a few on their own. Here's the list Donna wrote down:

- *What happened to immigrants on Ellis Island?*
- *Did all immigrants to the United States have to stop at Ellis Island?*
- *At Ellis Island, would any people not be allowed to enter the United States? Would they have to go back? Who?*
- *Why did immigrants stop going through Ellis Island?*
- *What goes on at Ellis Island today?*

Finding and Evaluating Books with More Information

While a good encyclopedia or another general reference book such as an **almanac** provides a good start and raises important research questions, it is not enough. Students need to locate additional sources of information. In the public library, Donna used the computerized catalog to see if she could find a nonfiction book about Ellis Island. (In some communities, library users can connect with the library's catalog from their home computer, search for books on a certain subject, and even find out whether the book is currently in the library or on loan to someone else.)

In the catalog, Donna found a listing for a book called *If Your Name Was Changed at Ellis Island*. The catalog entry also said that the author was Ellen Levine, that the book came out in 1993, and that the book belonged in the children's room. Donna knew the book belonged in the children's room because its call number included the letters JUV for "juvenile." (Most students learn in school that the **call number** is a combination of letters and numerals that appears on the catalog listing and on the spine of the book.) By looking at a map of the children's room in the library, Donna figured out which shelf to check for the book with the call number JUV 325.1.

Donna was pleased to find Ellen Levine's book about Ellis Island just where it belonged. She spent a few minutes looking over the **table of contents** and the **index** to see whether it dealt with her research questions. Next, she read a couple of pages to make sure the book was the right level for her. Finally, she used her library card to borrow the book.

Finding and Evaluating Sources on the Internet

On one of the computers in her classroom, Donna used a few **search engines,** such as the one at www.yahoo.com, to identify Web sites with information about Ellis Island. The search engines listed so many sites that Donna wasn't sure how to proceed. She decided to start at the top of the list and read the description of each site that dealt with Ellis Island. Based on the descriptions, she clicked on two Web addresses, or URLs.

One site belonged to the company that runs the Ellis Island Immigration Museum; she liked the way this site broke down the information into easy-to-follow sections, so she printed out some pages from the site, www.ellisisland.com. The other site looked useful at first glance but did not identify who created it, and it was partially "under construction"; Donna decided not to trust the information on this site. (Generally, the information in books and magazines is carefully checked before the works are published. Many Web sites, however, present information that no one checks; the information may be incorrect or intentionally misleading.)

Finding and Evaluating Other Sources of Information

Brainstorming with her classmates, her teacher, and her parents, Donna planned to watch, read, and interview three other sources as well:

- A rebroadcast of a program about the original hospital at Ellis Island and the immigrants who went there
- An editorial, "Ghosts of Ellis Island," which appeared in the *New York Times* on September 8, 2001
- Donna's cousin, who visited Ellis Island last year

The I-Search Report (continued)

Meanwhile, Danny's research into immigration continued on a very personal note. He already had his research questions. They came from his own curiosity about his family history. He started to find answers by using the passenger database from an Ellis Island Web site, www.ellisisland.org. Danny located important information that no other living person in his family seemed to have. He found out that a nineteen-year-old named Benjamin Corner from the city of Bucharest had arrived at Ellis Island on November 25, 1903, aboard the ship *Neckar,* which had sailed from Bremen, Germany. Could this be his grandmother's grandfather? What could he learn about him besides his date of arrival and his home town?

Danny's mother suggested that Danny search through shoeboxes of old photographs she had from 1910 to 1940. She also arranged for Danny to visit a ninety-five-year-old relative who remembered Benjamin Corner when he was a young man starting a new life in the United States. Finally, Danny realized he should find books or articles about life in Bucharest in the 1890s, when Benjamin was growing up there.

STAGE 3: KEEPING TRACK OF SOURCES

The teacher had reminded Donna, Danny, and the rest of the class that a research report gives the reader information about each source that the writer of the report used. She gave the students the following handout. It tells what kind of information the writer of the report must give the reader and includes examples for different kinds of sources. Many teachers don't require all this information from elementary- and middle-school students, but we give it here just in case the teacher wants it. After the handouts, we discuss *where* students should write all this information down.

Ms. Chin, January 2, 2002

HOW TO LIST SOURCES

When you find a source you will use to write your research report, look for the following information about the source. Some sources won't have all the information.

See the next page for examples of how you should write down all the information about each source.

- **Author's name:** For any source, give the name of a writer if possible. Give the writer's last name first. For a TV program, movie, other performance, or personal interview, you can give the name of the director, the producer, or the interviewee instead of the name of an author. (If the source does not list the name of any person who created it, begin with the title of the source.)
- **Title of source:** For any source, give its title.
- **More about the source:** For a book, put the city in which the publisher is located before the publisher's name. For an article in a newspaper or magazine, give the name of the newspaper or magazine and then the date on which the article was published. For a television program, give the name of the television station.
- **Date:** For a book or a magazine or newspaper article, give the date on which the item was published. For a television program, give the date on which the program played. For a Web site, give the date on which the site opened or was updated.

Ms. Chin, January 2, 2002

HOW TO LIST SOURCES
(continued)

Here are examples of how to write out the information you have collected for each source. On the page headed "Sources" at the end of your research report, list the sources in alphabetical order.

FOR AN ENCYCLOPEDIA
"Tubman, Harriet." The Grolier Multimedia
   Encyclopedia, 1995 ed.

FOR A BOOK (last name of author first)
Astarte, Frank. True Adventures on the High Seas.
   New York: Sea Stories Press, 1985.

FOR AN ARTICLE FROM A NEWSPAPER OR A MAGAZINE
Prial, Frank J. "New Life for Old Trolleys." New York
   Times, Dec. 9, 2001.

FOR A TELEVISION SHOW OR A MOVIE
Harris, Mark Jonathan. Into the Arms of Strangers:
   Stories of the Kindertransport. HBO, Dec. 9, 2001.

FOR A WEB SITE
"Ellis Island History."
   www.ellisisland.com/inspection.html, Dec. 1998.

FOR AN INTERVIEW
Clinton, Hillary Rodham. Personal interview, Dec. 9,
   2001.

The teacher told Donna, Danny, and the rest of the class that there are two places they can write down all the facts about their sources. The first place is on index cards. She showed how to put the information about each source on a separate index card, or **source card,** and how to number the source cards. Here are two examples.

"Ellis Island History." www.ellisisland.com/inspection.html.
Dec. 1998.

#1

Card with information about source #1

Astarte, Frank. <u>True Adventures on the High Seas.</u> New York: Sea Stories
Press, 1985.

#2

Card with information about source #2

Alternatively, a student can write down all the information about sources on a large chart, which he or she can also use for taking notes from each source. An example of such a chart appears later in this chapter.

After the student has drafted the report, he or she will have to transfer all the information about the sources to the end of the report. As Ms. Chin said on the handout, the student should put the heading "Sources" on the last page of the report and list the sources in alphabetical order.

The I-Search Report (continued)

Danny spent an afternoon talking to his great-great-aunt and making audio recordings of her memories of Benjamin Corner. She even played a record of Romanian music that she and Benjamin had listened to in the 1920s. Danny recorded part of the album so that his classmates could hear the music. Then Danny went on to read and take notes from printed sources about Bucharest, Romania, in the late nineteenth century.

Danny made source cards for books he was reading. He also made source cards for people he had spoken to and music he had heard.

STAGE 4: TAKING NOTES FROM THE SOURCES

Donna and Danny both needed to read or listen to each of their sources closely and to note how each source answered one or more of their research questions. Their teacher had taught the class two systems for taking notes.

Taking Notes on Index Cards

The researcher who uses this system should start out with a pile of fresh index cards to use as **note cards.** He or she should write one of his or her research questions at the top of each note card. When the researcher finds an answer in one of the sources, he or she should write that answer on the card. Next to the answer, the researcher should write the number of the source that appears on the source card.

The best way for a researcher to take notes is to paraphrase. To **paraphrase,** a researcher writes down the information from a source *in his or her own words.* Some notes can even take the form of incomplete sentences containing only key words. For example, if Donna read in a source, "Ellis Island was a United States immigration station for more than 60 years. During that time, officials examined more than 16 million aliens at the island," she could have written on a note card, "Used for 60+ years. More than 16 million aliens."

When it comes time to write her report, the facts just mentioned will appear in Donna's own words—not in words copied from the source. Teachers much prefer to get a report with the student's own words than a report made up of quotations from the student's sources. Only very rarely, if at all, should a student use the exact words of another writer and then only under two strict conditions: (1) the student must enclose the quoted words in quotation marks; (2) the student must give the name of the author and the title of the source that the quotation comes from.

We cannot stress the following enough: if a student or an adult uses the exact words of a source *without* putting them in quotation marks and *without* telling who wrote them originally, the student or adult is **plagiarizing,** or stealing. Plagiarism is strictly forbidden! The way to avoid plagiarism is to paraphrase. If the exact words from a source make their way without quotation marks onto a note card, chances are they will find their way into the final report. Again: students should work hard to avoid plagiarism.

Taking Notes on a Chart

This system is recommended by Elizabeth James and Carol Barkin in their book, *How to Write Super School Reports* (Lothrop, Lee & Shepard, 1998). The researcher who uses this system should write his or her research questions in columns across the top of the chart. The researcher has already listed the sources in the left-hand column. So now the chart will have columns and rows, with one box for what, if anything, each source says about each question. (See next page for an example of such a chart.)

Example of Notes from a Source

Here's a part of one of Donna's sources. Following it is an example of a filled-in note card based on the source.

Donna's Source

. . . doctors had only a few seconds to examine each immigrant, checking for sixty symptoms, from anemia to varicose veins, which might indicate a wide variety of diseases. . . . The disease which resulted in the most exclusions . . . was trachoma, a highly contagious eye infection that could cause blindness and death. . . . Physicians checked for trachoma by turning the eyelid inside out with their fingers, a hairpin, or a buttonhook to look for inflammations on the inner eyelid—a short but extremely painful experience. . . .

—from www.ellisisland.com/inspection.html

A Note Card with Note Based on the Source

Research question

What happened to immigrants on Ellis Island?

Paraphrase from source and number of source

Doctors checked immigrants for diseases—for example, eye disease called trachoma. Docs turned person's eyelid inside out. Used fingers or tool like hook. Could hurt patient.   #1

CHART WITH DONNA'S SOURCES, RESEARCH QUESTIONS, AND SOME NOTES

	What happened to immigrants on Ellis Island?	Did all immigrants to America have to stop at Ellis Island?	At Ellis Island, would any people not be allowed to enter the United States? Would they have to go back? Who?	Why did immigrants stop going through Ellis Island?	What goes on at Ellis Island today?
"Ellis Island History." www.ellisisland.com/inspection.html, Dec. 1998.	Doctors checked immigrants for diseases—for example, eye disease called trachoma. Docs turned person's eyelid inside out. Used fingers or tool like hook. Could hurt patient.			Number of immigrants went down	
Levine, Ellen. If Your Name Was Changed at Ellis Island. New York: Scholastic, 1993.					
"Ellis Island Hospital." HealthWeek. WLIW, Dec. 8, 2001.					
"Ghosts of Ellis Island." New York Times, Sept. 8, 2001.				Reception center no longer needed because fewer immigrants	
Diaz, Linda. Personal interview, Oct. 17, 2001.					

STAGE 5: DECIDING ON KIND OF PRESENTATION

Most of the time, teachers ask students who go through the research process to submit a written report. Donna, for example, intended to hand in a written report. Sometimes, though, teachers ask for or might welcome another form of presentation—perhaps an oral report with visual aids, a poster or videotaped presentation, or a Web site.

The I-Search Report (continued)

Because his research had turned up both music and pictures that related to Great-Great-Grandfather Benjamin's life, Danny decided that he should present his project as a videotape. That way, he could share the results of his research with his great-great-aunt, save the results for future generations, and also hand his teacher a product that she could evaluate and grade.

STAGE 6: ORGANIZING AND DRAFTING A WRITTEN RESEARCH REPORT

As noted earlier, some teachers give students a list of questions to be answered in a particular order. Many other teachers, however, expect students to organize their reports on their own. In such cases, students need to figure out a sensible order for presenting their findings and then to write up those findings in a few pages. When Donna filled in her chart more and studied it, she decided that she would not take up her questions in the order in which she had placed them on the chart. Rather, she felt her report would make more sense if she put the second question first. She prepared an **outline** to follow. (See Donna's outline on the following page.)

INTRODUCTION

1. *Immigrants who went through Ellis Island (not everyone)*
2. *Process those immigrants had to go through*
3. *Reasons people were denied entry to U.S.*
4. *Reasons immigrants no longer go through process on Ellis Island*
5. *Ellis Island today*

CONCLUSION

For each of the five main topics in her outline, Donna would try to write at least one paragraph. She would figure out what to say in each paragraph based on the answers she wrote under each question on her chart. If answers from different sources contradicted each other, she'd have to decide which source to believe and why. Alternatively, if two sources disagreed, she might come right out and mention in her report the disagreement between the sources.

Donna's first attempt at writing from her outline and notes will not be her final report. It will be her first draft. As noted in Chapter 1, "Paragraphs and Essays," no one expects a first draft to be perfect or even good enough to be handed in. After a student has completed the drafting stage of a report, he or she still has two more stages to go—making sure the report is in the proper format and fixing the report to make it a piece of writing that is ready for the teacher to see.

Writing an Opening Paragraph

As explained in Chapter 1, students need to understand that in an effective piece of writing, a strong introduction precedes the bulk of the piece, or the body. (In Donna's plan, the material numbered 1 to 5 makes up the body of the report.) The best kind of introduction is the one that pulls a reader right into the writing. Therefore, some writers begin with unusual facts or other means to make the reader think, "Wow! I've got to see what this is all about." Donna might, for example, begin her report by paraphrasing the claim by several of her sources that 40 percent of the people who live in the United States today are descended from a relative who entered this country through Ellis Island. Donna's opening paragraph might then go on to explain how her source or sources came up with that percentage and the significance of the fact.

Writing a Concluding Paragraph

Similarly, students need to appreciate the power of a strong conclusion after the body of the report. When the end of a piece of writing dribbles off, readers feel cheated. On the other hand, readers feel satisfied when a report ends by summing itself up or by explaining why reading the report was a good use of time. If a teacher allows the use of the pronoun I, students may want to end their reports by telling readers why writing this report was meaningful to them.

Listing Sources

A researcher must identify which sources he or she used to prepare the report. One of the main reasons teachers assign research reports is to teach students where to find information, how to use the information, and how to give credit to the people or organizations that provided the information.

The last part of a research report is a list of the sources the student has used. Some teachers will specify a minimum number of sources students must use—at least three is usual. Most teachers will give students a specific format they want them to use for listing their sources. (For the standard format, see the handout from Donna's teacher, Ms. Chin, earlier in this chapter.) Here's an example of the page listing all Donna's sources—in alphabetical order, as the teacher requested.

Sources

Diaz, Linda. Personal interview, Oct. 17, 2001.

"Ellis Island History." www.ellisisland.com/inspection.html, Dec. 1998.

"Ellis Island Hospital." <u>Healthweek.</u> WLIW, Dec. 8, 2001.

"Ghosts of Ellis Island." <u>New York Times,</u> Sept. 8, 2001.

Levine, Ellen. <u>If Your Name Was Changed at Ellis Island.</u> New York: Scholastic, 1993.

STAGE 7: FORMATTING A WRITTEN RESEARCH REPORT

For a written report, a student needs to check that he or she is using the format the teacher asked for. Did the teacher announce a preference on any of the following matters?

- Handwriting (pencil or pen) versus typing or word processing?
- Single- or double-spaced?
- Writing on one side or both sides of the paper?
- Position of heading (with name, class, date, anything else requested)?
- Size of margins?
- Separate cover or title page?
- Length of report (number of words or pages)
- Illustrations?
- List of sources on a separate page? Sources in alphabetical order?
- Number of sources to consult and to list at the end of report?

If the teacher did announce preferences, the student should be sure to follow the teacher's instructions. If the teacher did not announce format preferences, the student may make decisions for himself or herself. Whatever the format, the report should look attractive and presentable.

STAGE 8: IMPROVING AND FIXING: REVISING, EDITING, AND PROOFREADING A RESEARCH REPORT

After drafting a research report, the writer should put it away for at least a day. Then he or she should look at the report again, expecting to make some changes in both content and style. (See Chapter 1 for specific suggestions for fixing a piece of writing.) Before the writer submits a research report to the teacher, he or she should also ask someone else to read the report and give comments, or feedback.

At this point, writers who have spent time and energy in going through the eight stages discussed in this chapter deserve congratulations for tackling such a project and seeing it through. Their experience will help them enormously as they face research assignments in secondary school, in higher education, and, outside school, in the "real world."

! Implications

> To answer the question, "Why does all this matter?" or "What does it mean?," share the following insights with your child.

- **Writing a research report isn't easy, but it doesn't have to be painful.** An assignment to write a research report can sound like a pain. After all, a student has to go to the library, read a lot of books, take all those notes . . . and all that before he or she even sits down to write. But, like many things in life, if a student approaches this the right way, it's not all that hard. The key is to get started *right away* instead of putting the assignment off until the number of days before the due date do not equal the number of days needed to do the assignment. Then the student should take it one stage at a time. That's how people get big jobs done—they break them down into a series of smaller ones.

- **Students might actually enjoy writing a research report!**   After all, what is the student really being asked to do? The teacher wants the student to think of a topic that interests him or her and find out more about it. If at all possible, the student should find a topic that he or she really *is* interested in. But even if a student doesn't have a choice, he or she should give the topic a chance. Sometimes a researcher doesn't know how interesting a subject is until he or she starts learning about it. So it's important to keep an open mind.

- **It's good to be an expert.**   One reward a student gets from writing a research paper—besides the relief of finishing—is really getting to know a lot about one particular subject. It's very possible that, after a student has done research and written about it, he or she will know more about the topic than anyone else in the class—even the teacher. Being an expert on a topic and being able to speak in a knowledgeable way about it can be very satisfying!

Skills Practice

> The following activities give your child practice in applying the skills basic to writing research reports. For some of the activities, your child may need to review the information in the preceding pages.

A.   GENERATING RESEARCH QUESTIONS

> Have your child read the following source material as if he or she were beginning research for a report about the *Titanic*. Have your child use the information to generate research questions for the report.

Suppose you had to write a research report about the *Titanic*. The following passage is similar to one you would find in an encyclopedia—the first book you might use to begin your research. Based on this information, make up two research questions that you would try to answer by looking in additional sources.

The Titanic was a British steamship that was, when it was built, the largest ship in the world. It was thought to be unsinkable, but during its first trip, from England to New York City, on the night of April 14, 1912, it struck an iceberg and sank. Most of the passengers and crew died in the accident.

Suggested Answers

Why did people think the Titanic was unsinkable?

How come so many people were killed?

How come the ship hit the iceberg?

(Accept any reasonable answers.)

> **Evaluating Your Child's Skills:** The research questions should show that your child thought about the information presented and went on to ask questions about why and how the *Titanic* sank and what were the results of the accident. If your child has trouble, model one or two questions for him or her.

B.   WRITING SOURCE CARDS

> With your child, review the instructions and models for writing source cards for books and other sources. Then have your child practice writing source cards.

Write source cards for the following:

- A book called *The Titanic*, written by Deborah Kent, and published by Children's Press in New York in 1993.
- A Web site called Story of the Titanic with the Web address www.titanicstory.com/html. The article was put on the Web site on April 4, 2002.

If you don't have index cards, you can write on a sheet of paper instead. Don't forget to number your sources.

Answers

Kent, Deborah. <u>The Titanic</u>. New York: Children's Press, 1993.

#1

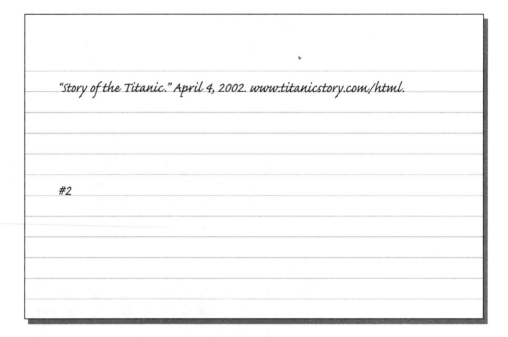

"Story of the Titanic." April 4, 2002. www.titanicstory.com/html.

#2

Evaluating Your Child's Skills: Be sure your child has used the correct format for citing sources. Check his or her answers with the sample source cards provided in this chapter.

C.   WRITING NOTE CARDS

Have your child read the sample information that might appear in a source and then write notes based on the information.

The source for the following information is from the Web site about the *Titanic* (source #2). Write note cards that answer the following two research questions:

• What made the *Titanic* sink?
• How come more people didn't survive the sinking of the *Titanic?*

The crew saw the iceberg before the crash, but it was too late to avoid it. The iceberg tore a 300-foot hole in the ship, and the *Titanic* sank in about 2½ hours. Approximately 2,200 people were on board, and there were enough lifeboats for less than half of them. Only 705 survived.

Suggested Answers

What made the _Titanic_ sink?

Titanic hit an iceberg. Crew saw iceberg too late to save ship. Iceberg made 300-foot hole in ship.   #2

How come more people didn't survive the sinking of the _Titanic_?

2,200 people on ship but not enough lifeboats. Room in lifeboats for less than half the people. Only 705 survivors.   #2

Evaluating Your Child's Skills: Check that your child has written the research question at the top of each card and included the source number on the card. Also check that the notes answer the research question. Most important, your child should paraphrase the information from the source—not copy the actual wording.

Top of the Class

> **If your child has mastered the basics of producing a well-researched, well-written report, he or she may appreciate some pointers on how to add one or more features that will make his or her research report really stand out.**

A. INCLUDE PICTURES

> **Your child can add visual interest to his or her report by including illustrations photocopied from printed material or downloaded from the Web.**

There's no substitute for good research and good writing. However, everyone enjoys attractive pictures. You may find a few pictures to photocopy from books, but the easiest way to get illustrations for your report is to find them on the Web and print them out. If you've done an I-Search report, you may have personal photographs that could really make your report come alive. Make sure the pictures you use aren't just for decoration; they should add meaning to your report by illustrating facts and concepts you've written about. One more thing—don't get carried away. Too many pictures could make your report look babyish. But one or two good ones could make a good report even better.

B. INCLUDE CHARTS OR DIAGRAMS

> **Encourage your child to present some of the information in his or her report on a chart or some other type of graphic organizer if any part of the report lends itself to this type of presentation.**

If you are including the kind of information that shows up well on a chart or table, you might want to include one. Your teacher will see that you really thought hard about the best way to present your facts, and a chart or table works like a picture to make a report more interesting to look at. Here are some types of information with a few suggestions for presentation. You can make the visuals by hand or on a computer.

Type of Information	Type of Presentation
Events that occurred on dates during a particular time period	Timeline
How something is divided up into different parts	Pie chart (circle divided into wedge-shaped sections)
How several different things can be described	Chart (names of things in left column, descriptions in right column)

Writer's Handbook

A Sample Social Studies Essay Test

On the following pages you will find part of a sampler of the test that New York State administers to fifth-grade students. The sampler is from June 2001. The part reproduced here, Part III, is an example of the essay question that students must answer based on their analysis of six documents. You can find the complete sampler at a part of the Web site of the New York State Education Department at www.emsc.nysed.gov/ciai/testing/samplerelint/elintsampsocst.html. Click on the part of the test you want to see. For help with answers for the sampler see www.emsc.nysed.gov/ciai/socst/pub/5samplerss2.pdf. (Other states have also adopted or are planning to adopt similar essay tests.)

Here's a letter from the New York State United Teachers. It offers advice to parents for helping their children with the state's fifth-grade test. The advice crosses state lines, of course.

September 27, 2000

Raising standards with DBQs

What do a map of Europe, an Army recruiting poster and some newspaper editorial cartoons have in common? They could be the basis for the answer your kids give to a Document-Based Question on the next social studies test.

Once found only on high school Advanced Placement tests, "DBQs" are working their way down to the elementary grades as the state moves to raise standards of teaching and learning in all schools.

As early as fifth grade, your children will be tested on their ability to analyze a collection of documents, tap their own knowledge and come up with reasoned answers to complex questions on multi-faceted topics.

It's a real-world skill they'll use all their lives.

Unfortunately, kids lose points on DBQs—and other tests, for that matter—because they don't focus on the details or the directions. Some simple steps can help you to help them develop their powers of observation. Above all, start these efforts early. After all, the DBQ your children will face on their fifth-grade social studies test is based on what they've learned from kindergarten through fourth grade.

Here are a few ways you can help give your kids the analytical skills they'll need to succeed at DBQs.

Elementary school and beyond

- Read to your kids and with them. Depending on their age, you can share observations from newsmagazines, newspapers and special-interest publications as well as books. Remember, DBQs test kids on their ability to analyze and understand many perspectives on the same issue.
- Quiz them on what they've read, but don't just have them parrot something back to you. Ask questions that require them to use critical-thinking skills.
- Encourage your child to compare and contrast toys, movies or books they have read. For example, discuss how toys have changed over time.

74

- You can teach even the youngest kids how a time line works by having them arrange family members by age or put the days of the week in order.
- Take advantage of the experiences—and priceless historical documents—available at New York's many museums and historical sites.

Middle school and beyond

- Share with your child an appropriate newspaper, magazine or TV advertisement and have the child explain the message. What is the advertiser trying to say? What is the advertiser really selling?
- The ability to read and understand maps and charts is important. On family trips, have the child draw a simple map or trace the route on a roadmap or atlas. Older children can take an active role as navigator.
- Visit an old cemetery and discuss the stories the headstones tell—How long did people live? Why did some children die so young? How have given names changed over the years?
- Help kids find their own documents around the house. Every family has old newspapers, family papers, home movies, photos and souvenirs to look at and discuss.
- Encourage your child to write whenever possible. Start a family journal and trade it back and forth on trips or during summer vacation.
- TV has much to offer if you exercise some control over what your children are watching. Spend some time on the many channels with history, science and news programming.
- Instead of asking "How was the movie?" help your child analyze a film or video they've just seen. What was the main idea of the film? What was the director trying to say?
- Just because your kids have grown up as part of a visual generation, it doesn't mean they know how to observe something. When looking at a painting, for instance, ask if the child knows what's going on in one corner of the work. Do the people in the painting represent something?

From www.nysut.org/newyorkteacher/resources/standards/parents-dbq.html.

PART III:
DOCUMENT-BASED QUESTION

Directions: The task below is based on documents 1 through 6. This task is designed to test your ability to work with historical documents. Look at each document and answer the question or questions after each document. Use your answers to the questions to help you write your essay.

Historical Background:

The building of the Erie Canal brought many changes for people in New York State. Once completed in 1825, the canal helped New York become the Empire State.

Task: For Part A, read *each* document carefully and answer the question or questions after each document. Then read the directions for Part B and write your essay.

For Part B, use your answers from Part A, information from the documents, and your knowledge of social studies to write a well-organized essay. In the essay you should:

> Explain *three* ways communities in New York State benefited from the building of the Erie Canal.

Document 1

Folk songs are stories set to music. The most famous Erie Canal song is "Low Bridge, Everybody Down," or "Fifteen Miles on the Erie Canal," by Thomas S. Allen.

> **Low Bridge, Everybody Down**
>
> I got a mule, her name is Sal,
> Fifteen miles on the Erie Canal!
> She's a good old worker and a good old pal,
> Fifteen miles on the Erie Canal!
> We've hauled some barges in our day,
> Filled with lumber, coal and hay,
> And we know ev'ry inch of the way
> From Albany to Buffalo
> (chorus)
> Low bridge, ev'rybody down,
> Low bridge, 'cause we're coming to town,
> And you'll always know your neighbor,
> You'll always know your pal,
> If you ever navigated on the Erie Canal. . . .

1. According to this song, name two products that were shipped on the Erie Canal.

   a. _____ [1]

   b. _____ [1]

Document 2

Before the building of the Erie Canal, most people in New York State had settled in New York City and along the Hudson River. However, west of that area was mostly wilderness. This changed when the canal opened.

[Today] with the exception of Binghamton and Elmira, every major city in New York falls along the trade route established by the Erie Canal, from New York City to Albany, through Schenectady, Utica, and Syracuse, to Rochester and Buffalo. Approximately 75% of the State's population still lives within the corridors created by the waterways of the New York State canal system and the Hudson River Valley.

Route of the Erie Canal

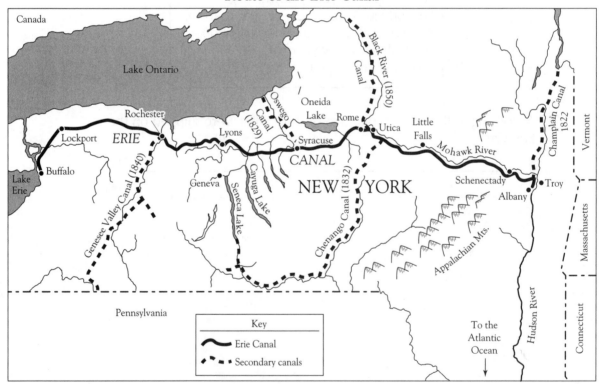

1. According to the reading passage and the map, how did the Erie Canal help the growth of New York State west of the Hudson River? _____ _____ _____ [1]

Document 3

The Erie Canal affected the population of New York State. Look at the census (population) data for Albany, New York City, and Buffalo between 1820 and 1880.

POPULATIONS OF THREE CITIES IN NEW YORK STATE, 1820–1880

Years	Population of Albany	Population of New York City	Population of Buffalo
1820	12,630	123,706	2,095
1830	24,209	202,589	8,668
1840	33,721	312,710	18,213
1850	50,763	515,547	42,261
1860	62,367	813,669	81,129
1870	76,216	942,292	111,714
1880	90,758	1,206,299	115,134

1. Complete the chart with the population numbers of these *three* cities in 1820, 1840, and 1870.

	1820	1840	1870
a. Albany	12,630		
b. New York City			942,292
c. Buffalo		18,213	

2. How did the population change in these three cities during the period from 1820 to 1870? _____

_____

_____ [1]

Document 4

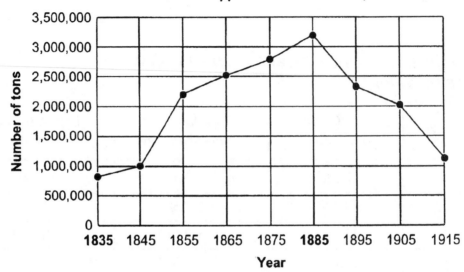

Tons of Goods Shipped on the Erie Canal, 1835–1915

1. According to this line graph, how did the amount of goods shipped on the Erie Canal change between **1835** and **1885**? _____
_____
_____ [1]

Document 5

The following description, written in 1832, describes Buffalo, New York in spring once the ice was gone and the Erie Canal was reopened.

> Canal boats filled with emigrants, and covered with goods and furniture, are almost hourly arriving. The boats are discharged of their [human] freight [passengers], and for the time being, natives of all climates and countries [walk] our streets, either to satisfy their curiosity, purchase necessaries [goods], or to inquire [ask about] the most favorable points for their future location.

1. Based on this document, what did the canal boats often carry?

   _____
   _____ [1]

2. List **one** way communities, like Buffalo, benefited from people traveling along the Erie Canal.

   _____
   _____ [1]

Document 6

By 1825, the Erie Canal gave another boost to New York's already busy seaports. Commercial vessels could now travel north up the Hudson River all the way to Lake Erie. This new waterway connected the Atlantic Ocean to the Great Lakes, and it caused a terrific boom [increase] in industry all along the Hudson River and made New York's ports and harbor more valuable than ever.

Between 1830 and 1860, New York City and its seaport grew at an astounding rate. "Prior to the construction of the canal, New York City was the nation's fifth largest seaport, behind Boston, Baltimore, Philadelphia, and New Orleans. Within 15 years of the opening of Erie Canal, New York was the busiest port in America, moving [more goods] than Boston, Baltimore, and New Orleans combined."

1. According to this document, list **two** effects the Erie Canal had on New York City.

   a. _____

   _____

   _____ [1]

   b. _____

   _____

   _____ [1]

PART III: DOCUMENT-BASED QUESTION
PART B—ESSAY

Directions: Using the documents, the answers to the questions in Part A, and your knowledge of social studies, write a well-organized essay.

Historical Background: The building of the Erie Canal brought many changes for people in New York State. Once completed in 1825, the canal helped New York become the Empire State.

Task:

> Explain **three** ways communities in New York State benefited from the building of the Erie Canal.

In your essay remember to:

- Explain **three** ways communities in New York State benefited from the building of the Erie Canal.
- Include an introduction, a body, and a conclusion.
- Use information from the documents in your answer.
- Include details, examples, or reasons in developing your ideas.

Planning Page

You may plan your writing for the essay on this page but do not write your final essay here. Your writing on this page will not count toward your final score.

Spelling Rules and Tips

One way to write an essay or report that appears correct and polished is to make sure that all words are spelled correctly. Because most words in English follow regular spelling rules, you can use these rules to avoid spelling errors and, later, to correct errors. The most important of these rules appear in the chart that follows. (Note that some words are hard to spell and must simply be memorized. These words are exceptions to the rules. Some of them are noted here along with examples of words that do follow the rules.)

Adding Suffixes to Words That End with Silent e

Spelling Rules	Examples and Common Exceptions
To add -ly to a word that ends with l plus silent e, always drop the le.	**Examples:** wobble + -ly = wobbly able + -ly = -ably **Exception:** whole + -ly = wholly (drop the e and double the l.)
To add any other suffix that begins with a consonant to a word that ends with silent e, do not drop the e.	**Examples:** care + -ful = careful like + -ly = likely whole + -some = wholesome **Exceptions:** argue + -ment = argument awe + -ful = awful
To add a suffix that begins with a vowel or y to a word that ends with silent e, usually drop the e.	**Examples:** lace + -y = lacy survive + -al = survival move + -ing = moving
To add a suffix that begins with a or o to a word that ends with ce or ge, do not drop the e. (Dropping the e would change the sound of the c or g from "soft" to "hard.")	**Examples:** change + -able = changeable courage + -ous = courageous replace + -able = replaceable
To add a suffix that begins with a vowel to a word that ends with ee or oe, keep the e.	disagree + -able = disagreeable hoe + -ing = hoeing

Adding Suffixes to Words That End with y

Spelling Rules	Examples
If a word ends with a consonant + *y*, change the *y* to *i*.	try + -ed = tried rely + -es = relies
If a suffix begins with an *i*, do not change the *y* to *i*.	try + -ing = trying rely + -ing = relying
If a word ends with a vowel + *y*, do not drop the *y*.	play + -ful = playful annoy + -ed = annoyed

Using the Letters ie and ei

Use this simple rhyming rule to remember how to place the letters *ie* and *ei* in words: *i* before *e* except after *c* and when sounded like *a*, as in *neighbor* and *weigh*.

Spelling Rules	Examples
In most words, put *i* before *e*.	believe, sieve, relief
Put *e* before *i* after the letter *c*.	deceive, deceit, receive
Put *e* before *i* to sound like *a*, as in *neighbor* and *weigh*.	beige, eight, weight
Exceptions: There are only seven words that do not follow the rule.	either, height, leisure, neither, seize, species, weird

Doubling a Final Consonant

If a word ends with a consonant, it may be necessary to double the final consonant when adding a suffix.

DOUBLE THE FINAL CONSONANT if a word **ends in a single consonant following one vowel** AND

- the word has only one syllable

  Examples: bat + -er = batter

  sit + -ing = sitting

  mad + -er = madder

- the last syllable of the word is accented and the accent remains after the suffix is added

   Examples: occur + ing = occurring

                  prefer + ed = preferred

                  control + -able = controllable

DO NOT DOUBLE THE FINAL CONSONANT if

- the suffix begins with a consonant

   Examples: warm + -ly = warmly

                  pain + -less = painless

- the accent is not on the last syllable

   Examples: interest + -ing = interesting

                  linger + ed = lingered

                  instant + -ly = instantly

- the accent changes when the suffix is added

   Examples: prefer + -able = preferable

                  refer + -ence = reference

- two vowels come before the final consonant

   Examples: lean + -ed = leaned

                  fool + -ing = fooling

                  train + -er = trainer

- the word ends with two consonants

   Examples: find + -ing = finding

                  paint + -ed = painted

Remember: If a word ends in *ll* and the suffix *-ly* is added, drop one *l*.

    Examples: full + -ly = fully

                    dull + -ly = dully

Forming Compound Words

A compound word is a word such as *playground* that is formed from two words. To join two words to form a compound word, keep the original spelling of both words.

    Examples: baseball

                    haircut

                    homework

Forming Plurals

To form the plurals of most nouns in English, add *-s* or *-es*. On the following chart, you will find general rules that tell when to add *-e* and when to add *-es*.

General Rules for Plurals	*Examples*
If a noun ends with s, *ch*, *sh*, *x*, or *z*, add *es*.	boss → bosses batch → batches wish → wishes box → boxes buzz → buzzes
If a noun ends with a consonant + *y*, change y to *i* and add *-es*.	cherry → cherries puppy → puppies lady → ladies
If a noun ends with a vowel + *y*, add *-s*	day → days toy → toys key → keys
If a noun ends with a vowel + *o*, add *-s*	studio → studios patio → patios radio → radios
If a noun ends with a consonant + *o*, usually add *-s*.	piano → pianos solo → solos **Exceptions:** potato → potatoes hero → heroes echo → echoes
If a noun ends with *f* or *ff*, add *-s*	cliff → cliffs roof → roofs cuff → cuffs **Exceptions:** thief → thieves loaf → loaves
If a noun ends with *lf*, change *f* to *v*, and add *-es*.	half → halves wolf → wolves elf → elves
If a noun ends with *fe*, change *f* to *v* and add *-s*.	wife → wives knife → knives

On the following chart, you will find special rules for plurals.

Special Rules for Plurals	Examples
To form the plurals of most proper names, add -s. Add -es if the name ends in s, ch, sh, x, or z.	Washington → Washingtons Jones → Joneses Beach → Beaches Rush → Rushes Marx → Marxes Schwartz → Schwartzes
To form the plurals of one-word compound nouns, follow the general rules for plurals.	playground → playgrounds icebox → iceboxes meatloaf → meatloaves strawberry → strawberries
To form the plurals of hyphenated compound nouns or two-or-more-word compound nouns, make the most important word plural.	sister-in-law → sisters-in-law chief of staff → chiefs of staff
Some nouns have irregular plural forms. They do not follow any rules, so you have to memorize them.	woman → women mouse → mice foot → feet
Some nouns are spelled the same whether they are singular or plural.	sheep → sheep deer → deer series → series

Use the Dictionary

If you are not sure how to spell a word, look it up in a dictionary. You might ask, "How can I look up a word if I don't know how to spell it in the first place?" Here is how:

1. Write down all the ways you think the word could be spelled.
2. Search for each of these possible spellings in the dictionary.

Avoiding Sexist Language

Years ago, the words *he, his,* and *him* were accepted as general pronouns to refer to any person whose gender was unknown. In other words, the following sentence was considered correct:

Everyone in the class should hand in his report by Monday morning.

Now, that sentence would be acceptable only if all the students in the class were male. Using a masculine pronoun to include people who might be female is no longer acceptable. It is considered an example of using **sexist language,** or language that "prefers" males over females. The sentence could be improved by rewording it as follows:

Everyone in the class should hand in his or her report by Monday morning.

But if you use phrases such as "him or her," "he or she," and "his or hers" over and over again, your writing begins to sound awkward and repetitive. Sometimes you have to use these phrases, but you can often avoid them by using plurals—*they, them,* and *their* or *theirs.* The sentence about the report would be even better reworded as follows:

All students in the class should hand in their reports by Monday morning.

Another alternative is to avoid using a pronoun altogether:

All reports are due on Monday morning.

The use of male pronouns is not the only example of sexist language. There are others. Sexist language is not acceptable in your essays and reports. The following checklist will help you avoid using it.

- Do not mention a person's gender at all if it is not important to know whether the person is male or female.

  Sexist: male nurse, female scientist

  Substitutes: nurse, scientist

- Do not use language that stereotypes certain occupations. For example, do not use *she* or *her* when writing about a teacher who might be male. Do not use *he* or *him* when writing about a doctor who might be female. In general, do not assume that all people who have a certain job or position are of one gender or the other.

  Sexist: A doctor should treat his patients kindly.

  Substitutes: A doctor should treat his or her patients kindly.

                      Doctors should treat their patients kindly.

  Sexist: All mothers should pick up their children by 3:00.

  Substitute: All parents should pick up their children by 3:00.

- Do not use words ending in *man* or *men* if they refer to people who may be female.

  Sexist: fireman, policeman

  Substitutes: firefighter, police officer

The following chart suggests additional substitutes for "man" words:

Example of Sexist Language	*Substitute*
businessman	businessperson
chairman, chairwoman	chairperson
congressman	representative, member of Congress
mailman	mail carrier
mankind	humankind, humanity, the human race
workman	worker
salesman	salesperson

How to Read a Dictionary Entry

A dictionary is an essential tool for writers who are responding to assignments in social studies and other subjects. This important reference book contains entries in alphabetical order. After each entry word or phrase, a dictionary gives its pronunciation, meaning or meanings, and other information. You will find that a dictionary tells you much more than meanings of its entries.

Depending on the level of dictionary you use, you will find an entry as simple as the first example here or as detailed as the second example.

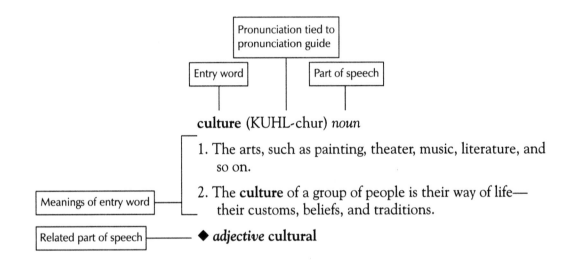

culture (KUHL-chur) *noun*

1. The arts, such as painting, theater, music, literature, and so on.

2. The **culture** of a group of people is their way of life— their customs, beliefs, and traditions.

◆ *adjective* **cultural**

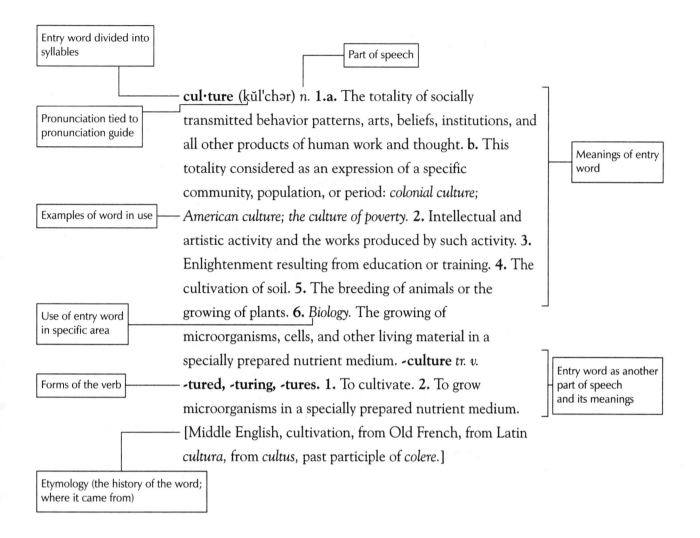

Entry word divided into syllables

Pronunciation tied to pronunciation guide

Examples of word in use

Use of entry word in specific area

Forms of the verb

Etymology (the history of the word; where it came from)

Part of speech

Meanings of entry word

Entry word as another part of speech and its meanings

cul·ture (kŭl'chər) *n.* **1.a.** The totality of socially transmitted behavior patterns, arts, beliefs, institutions, and all other products of human work and thought. **b.** This totality considered as an expression of a specific community, population, or period: *colonial culture; American culture; the culture of poverty.* **2.** Intellectual and artistic activity and the works produced by such activity. **3.** Enlightenment resulting from education or training. **4.** The cultivation of soil. **5.** The breeding of animals or the growing of plants. **6.** *Biology.* The growing of microorganisms, cells, and other living material in a specially prepared nutrient medium. **-culture** *tr. v.* **-tured, -turing, -tures. 1.** To cultivate. **2.** To grow microorganisms in a specially prepared nutrient medium. [Middle English, cultivation, from Old French, from Latin *cultura*, from *cultus*, past participle of *colere*.]

How to Read a Thesaurus Entry

One reason to use a dictionary (see page 92) is to find the meaning of a word. Sometimes you already know the meaning of a word, but you want to use a *better* word, a more appropriate word for what you are writing. At times like this, you can turn to a special type of dictionary called a thesaurus (thi SOR uhss).

Here's an example of how a thesaurus can help you. Of course, you know the meaning of the verb *speak,* but let's say you're looking for a synonym for *speak*—that is, for another word that means *speak* but that expresses a particular kind of speaking. You probably will recognize the synonym when you hear it or see it, but you just can't think of it right now. If you look in a thesaurus, here's what you might find. (We've added the boxed labels to help you figure out all the parts of the example.)

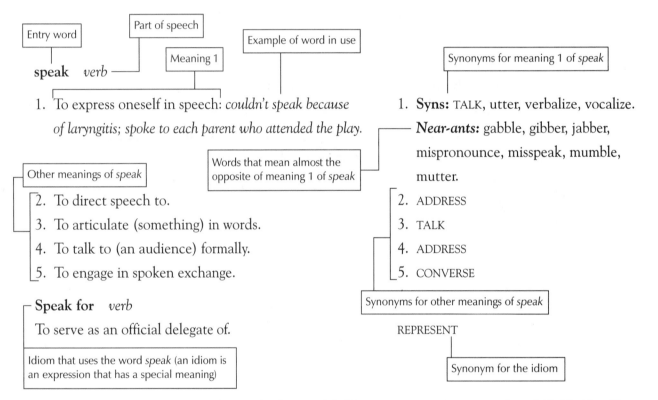

Example entry has been modified from a more complete entry in Roget's II: The New Thesaurus (Houghton Mifflin, 1988).

Based on this sample entry from a thesaurus, you may decide to use the word *address* or the word *converse* instead of the word *speak.* If you look up one of the synonyms in capital letters, you will find even more synonyms.

In general, it's not a good idea to put a synonym into your essay or report if you've never heard the word before. If a word is brand-new to you, you might use it in a way that's not quite right. Instead, use the thesaurus to help you find a synonym that you already know but just can't think of at the moment. In other words, let the thesaurus jog your brain.

Using the Library

The Internet is a wonderful research tool. But the chances are that you won't find all the information you need for a report on the Internet. You'll very likely need to use some good old-fashioned books as well. And that means that you'll be making at least one trip to the library. Once you get there, knowing your way around will help you to find what you need and to work quickly and efficiently. Start out in the children's room if you're an elementary-school student. If you're older, you may want to use the adult section instead.

Regardless of whether you're using the children's or the adult section, the first thing you need to know is where to find the catalog, whether it's on a computer or in a card file. The catalog in a library lists all the books the library has. It's where you go to find out if the library has the books you are looking for and which other books they have that will provide you with the information you need for your report. If you don't know where the catalog is or how to use it, ask a librarian to help you get started.

The way you use the catalog will depend on what you are looking for and the type of research you are doing. Suppose you already know the titles of one or more books you need for your report. Go straight to the catalog and look up the title or titles, using alphabetical order. Remember to look up titles under the first main word of the title—not *A* or *The*. For example, if you are looking for a book called *The Supreme Court*, look under *S* for *Supreme*, not under *T* for *The*. If you don't have a particular title in mind, but you know the name of one or more authors whose books you would like to use, look up the author's last name and see which titles are listed under his or her name. If you do not find a title listed in the catalog, the book is not in the library. You'll have to find other books to use instead. The same goes for authors.

But suppose you don't have specific titles or authors in mind. You just know what subject you need to research. Look up the subject in the catalog to find a list of books on that subject. If you are doing a research report about the Supreme Court, for example, look up *Supreme Court*. But if you are writing a report about Abraham Lincoln, look up *Lincoln, Abraham*. Always use a person's last name when using the library catalog unless, of course, the person's name is the title of the book. (If you are looking for a book that has the title *Abraham Lincoln*, you'll look under *A* for *Abraham*.)

Now that you know how to find out which books are available to you, let's talk about how to get your hands on those books. How do you find them on the shelves? If you are looking for a book of fiction, simply go to the fiction section, where books are arranged on the shelves in alphabetical order by authors' last names. If you want to use an encyclopedia, atlas, almanac, or another type of reference book, go to the reference section. But remember that you can't take books from the reference section home with you. You can use them only in the library, so be prepared to take notes.

Now suppose you're looking for a nonfiction book that is not a reference book. Let's go back to the catalog. Your library may use one of two systems to classify, or organize, books in the catalog. Most libraries use the **Dewey decimal system,** while others use the **Library of Congress system.** Look at the catalog listing for a title. Along with the title, author, and other information, you'll find one or more numbers if your library uses the Dewey decimal system. The numbers are called **call numbers.** If the library uses the Library of Congress system, you'll find one or more **call letters** instead. Those same numbers or letters are printed on the spine of the book you are looking for, and they will lead you right to the book because the books are arranged on the shelves in order of their call numbers or call letters. Books with the same combinations of numbers or letters are arranged alphabetically by authors' last names. Books with the same numbers by the same author are then arranged alphabetically by title.

The call numbers and call letters also let you know the general subject of a book. The following charts explain how books are classified by both the Dewey decimal and the Library of Congress systems.

DEWEY DECIMAL SYSTEM

Numbers	General Subject	Examples of Specific Subjects
000–099	general reference works	encyclopedias, atlases
100–199	philosophy	psychology, ideas
200–299	religion	myths, different religions
300–399	social sciences	politics, education
400–499	language	foreign language books
500–599	sciences	plants, animals, space
600–699	technology	computers, machines
700–799	arts	music, painting, sports
800–899	literature	poems, plays, essays
900–999	history and geography	ancient history, biography

LIBRARY OF CONGRESS SYSTEM

Letters	General Subject	Letters	General Subject
A	general works	M	music
B	philosophy and religion	N	art
C–F	history	P	language and literature
G	geography	Q	science
H	social sciences	R	medicine
J	politics	S	agriculture
K	law	T	technology
L	education	U	military science
		V	naval science
		Z	book lists and library science

If you know how your library's classification system works, you can often find books by just browsing. Say you're doing research for a report about trees, and say your library uses the Dewey decimal system. You know that the books numbered from 500 to 599 are about science, and within those numbers is a group of books that are about plants. If you look up and down the shelves in that area, you're bound to find books on your subject. Here's another way browsing can be useful. Suppose you have to do a science report, but you can't decide on a topic. Just browsing the shelves in the 500s section and looking at the titles may give you some ideas.

A library is a wonderful place, full of information and knowledge about every subject imaginable. If you know how to use it, you'll have a tool for success in all your school subjects—and a key to lifelong learning.

Table of Weights and Measures

Be sure to ask your teacher whether he or she wants you to use the **English system** of weights and measures (inches, quarts, pounds) or the **metric system** (centimeters, liters, kilograms) in your writing. Your teacher may want you to use both—one first and the other in parentheses, as in "The race was 6.2 miles (10 kilometers)." The following chart is called a **conversion table.** It makes it easy for you to figure out how to convert weights and measures from one system to the other. (Your results will be approximate, but close enough to be reasonably accurate. A calculator will make your work faster.)

LENGTH AND DISTANCE

When you know:	Multiply by:	To get:
inches	25	millimeters
feet	30	centimeters
yards	0.9	meters
miles	1.6	kilometers
millimeters	0.04	inches
centimeters	0.4	inches
meters	1.1	yards
kilometers	0.6	miles

SURFACE OR AREA

When you know:	Multiply by:	To get:
square inches	6.5	square centimeters
square feet	0.09	square meters
square yards	0.8	square meters
square miles	2.6	square kilometers
acres	0.4	hectares
square centimeters	0.16	square inches
square meters	1.2	square yards
square kilometers	0.4	square miles
hectares	2.5	acres

VOLUME AND CAPACITY (LIQUID)

When you know:	Multiply by:	To get:
fluid ounces	30	milliliters
pints	0.47	liters
quarts	0.95	liters
gallons	3.8	liters
milliliters	0.034	fluid ounces
liters	2.1	pints
liters	1.06	quarts
liters	0.26	gallons

WEIGHT

When you know:	Multiply by:	To get:
ounces	28	grams
pounds	0.45	kilograms
grams	0.035	ounces
kilograms	2.2	pounds

TEMPERATURE

When you know:	Multiply by:	To get:
degrees Fahrenheit	⅝ (after subtracting 32)	degrees Celsius
degrees Celsius	⅝ (then add 32)	degrees Fahrenheit

States of the Union

State	Date of entry (order)	Capital	Area sq mi/sq km	Population (April 1, 2000)	Nickname	Region
Alabama	1819 (22)	Montgomery	52,237/135,293	4,447,100	Heart of Dixie	Southeast
Alaska	1959 (49)	Juneau	615,230/1,593,444	626,932	Last Frontier	Separate
Arizona	1912 (48)	Phoenix	114,006/295,276	5,130,632	Grand Canyon State	Southwest
Arkansas	1836 (25)	Little Rock	53,182/137,742	2,673,400	Land of Opportunity	Southeast
California	1850 (31)	Sacramento	158,869/411,470	33,871,648	Golden State	West
Colorado	1876 (38)	Denver	104,100/269,618	4,301,261	Centennial State	West
Connecticut	1788 (5)	Hartford	5,544/14,358	3,405,565	Constitution State	New England
Delaware	1787 (1)	Dover	2,396/6,206	783,600	First State	Mid-Atlantic
Florida	1845 (27)	Tallahassee	59,928/155,214	15,982,378	Sunshine State	Southeast
Georgia	1788 (4)	Atlanta	58,977/152,750	8,186,453	Empire State of the South; Goober State; Peach State	Southeast
Hawaii	1959 (50)	Honolulu	6,459/16,729	1,211,537	Aloha State	Separate
Idaho	1890 (43)	Boise	83,574/216,456	1,293,953	Gem State	West
Illinois	1818 (21)	Springfield	57,918/150,007	12,419,293	Prairie State	Midwest
Indiana	1816 (19)	Indianapolis	36,420/94,328	6,080,485	Hoosier State	Midwest
Iowa	1846 (29)	Des Moines	56,276/145,754	2,926,324	Hawkeye State	Midwest
Kansas	1861 (34)	Topeka	82,282/213,110	2,688,418	Sunflower State	Midwest
Kentucky	1792 (15)	Frankfort	40,411/104,665	4,041,769	Bluegrass State	Southeast
Louisiana	1812 (18)	Baton Rouge	49,651/128,595	4,468,976	Pelican State	Southeast
Maine	1820 (23)	Augusta	33,741/97,388	1,274,923	Pine Tree State	New England
Maryland	1788 (7)	Annapolis	12,297/31,849	5,296,486	Free State; Old Line State	Mid-Atlantic
Massachusetts	1788 (6)	Boston	9,241/23,934	6,349,097	Bay State	New England
Michigan	1837 (26)	Lansing	96,705/250,465	9,938,444	Wolverine State	Midwest
Minnesota	1858 (32)	St. Paul	86,943/225,182	4,919,479	North Star State	Midwest
Mississippi	1817 (20)	Jackson	48,286/125,060	2,844,658	Magnolia State	Southeast
Missouri	1821 (24)	Jefferson City	69,709/180,546	5,595,211	Show Me State	Midwest
Montana	1889 (41)	Helena	147,046/380,849	902,195	Treasure State	West
Nebraska	1867 (37)	Lincoln	77,358/200,358	1,711,263	Cornhusker State	Midwest

State	Date of entry (order)	Capital	Area sq mi/sq km	Population (April 1, 2000)	Nickname	Region
Nevada	1864 (36)	Carson City	110,567/286,367	1,998,257	Silver State	West
New Hampshire	1788 (9)	Concord	9,283/24,044	1,235,786	Granite State	New England
New Jersey	1787 (3)	Trenton	8,215/21,277	8,414,350	Garden State	Mid-Atlantic
New Mexico	1912 (47)	Santa Fe	121,598/314,939	1,819,046	Land of Enchantment	Southwest
New York	1788 (11)	Albany	53,989/139,833	18,976,457	Empire State	Mid-Atlantic
North Carolina	1789 (12)	Raleigh	52,672/136,421	8,049,313	Tar Heel State	Southeast
North Dakota	1889 (39)	Bismarck	70,704/183,123	642,200	Peace Garden State; Flickertail State	Midwest
Ohio	1803 (17)	Columbus	44,828/116,103	11,353,140	Buckeye State	Midwest
Oklahoma	1907 (46)	Oklahoma City	69,903/181,048	3,450,654	Sooner State	Southwest
Oregon	1859 (33)	Salem	97,132/251,571	3,421,399	Beaver State	West
Pennsylvania	1787 (2)	Harrisburg	46,058/119,291	12,281,054	Keystone State	Mid-Atlantic
Rhode Island	1790 (13)	Providence	1,231/3,189	1,048,319	Ocean State	New England
South Carolina	1788 (8)	Columbia	31,189/80,779	4,012,012	Palmetto State	Southeast
South Dakota	1889 (40)	Pierre	77,121/199,744	754,844	Mount Rushmore State; Coyote State	Midwest
Tennessee	1796 (16)	Nashville	42,146/109,158	5,689,283	Volunteer State	Southeast
Texas	1845 (28)	Austin	267,277/692,248	20,851,820	Lone Star State	Southwest
Utah	1896 (45)	Salt Lake City	84,904/219,902	2,233,169	Beehive State	West
Vermont	1791 (14)	Montpelier	9,615/24,903	608,827	Green Mountain State	New England
Virginia	1788 (10)	Richmond	42,326/109,625	7,078,515	Old Dominion	Southeast
Washington	1889 (42)	Olympia	70,637/182,949	5,894,121	Evergreen State	West
West Virginia	1863 (35)	Charleston	24,231/62,759	1,808,344	Mountain State	Southeast
Wisconsin	1848 (30)	Madison	65,499/169,643	5,363,675	Badger State	Midwest
Wyoming	1890 (44)	Cheyenne	97,818/253,349	493,782	Equality State	West

Total area: Data from 1990 as reported in *Statistical Abstract of the United States, 2000.*
Resident population: U.S. Department of Commerce, U.S. Census Bureau.

Countries of the World

Country	Area sq mi/sq km	Population	Capital	Major languages	Continent
Afghanistan	251,772/652,089	24,800,000	Kabul	Pashtu and Afghan Persian	Asia
Albania	10,579/27,400	3,300,000	Tiranë	Albanian and Greek	Europe
Algeria	919,590/2,381,738	30,200,000	Algiers	Arabic, Berber, and French	Africa
Andorra	185/479	54,000	Andorra la Vella	Catalan, French, and Castilian Spanish	Europe
Angola	481,350/1,246,697	12,000,000	Luanda	Portuguese and Bantu	Africa
Antigua and Barbuda	170/440	100,000	St. John's	English	North America
Argentina	1,056,640/2,736,698	36,100,000	Buenos Aires	Spanish, English, and Italian	South America
Armenia	10,888/28,200	3,800,000	Yerevan	Armenian	Asia
Australia	2,951,521/7,644,439	18,700,000	Canberra	English and aboriginal languages	Australia
Austria	31,942/82,729	8,100,000	Vienna	German	Europe
Azerbaijan	33,436/86,599	7,700,000	Baku	Azeri, Russian, and Armenian	Asia
The Bahamas	3,860/9,997	300,000	Nassau	English and Creole	North America
Bahrain	266/689	600,000	Manama	Arabic, English, Farsi, and Urdu	Asia
Bangladesh	50,260/130,173	123,400,000	Dhaka	Bangla and English	Asia
Barbados	166/430	300,000	Bridgetown	English	North America
Belarus	80,108/207,480	10,200,000	Minsk	Byelorussian and Russian	Europe
Belgium	11,790/30,536	10,200,000	Brussels	Flemish and French	Europe
Belize	8,800/22,792	200,000	Belmopan	English and Spanish	North America
Benin	42,710/110,619	6,000,000	Porto-Novo	French and Fon	Africa
Bhutan	18,150/47,009	800,000	Thimphu	Dzongkha and Nepali	Asia
Bolivia	418,680/1,084,381	8,000,000	Sucre (judicial) and La Paz (administrative)	Spanish	South America

Country			Capital	Language	Continent
Bosnia and Herzegovina	16,691/43,320	4,000,000	Sarejevo	Serbo-Croatian	Europe
Botswana	218,810/566,718	1,400,000	Gaborone	English and Setswana	Africa
Brazil	3,265,060/8,456,505	162,100,000	Brasília	Portuguese, Spanish, French, and English	South America
Brunei	2,035/5,271	300,000	Bandar Seri Begawan	Malay, English, and Chinese	Asia
Bulgaria	42,683/110,548	8,300,000	Sofia	Bulgarian	Europe
Burkina Faso	105,637/273,763	11,300,000	Ouagadougou	French and Sudanic languages	Africa
Burundi	9,900/25,641	5,500,000	Bujumbura	Kurund, French, and Swahili	Africa
Cambodia	68,154/176,519	10,800,000	Phnom Penh	Khmer and French	Asia
Cameroon	179,690/465,397	14,300,000	Yaoundé	English and French	Africa
Canada	3,849,674/9,970,610	31,000,000	Ottawa	English and French	North America
Cape Verde	1,560/4,040	400,000	Praia	Portuguese	Africa
Central African Republic	240,530/622,973	3,400,000	Bangui	French and Sango	Africa
Chad	486,180/1,259,206	7,400,000	N'Djamena	French and Arabic	Africa
Chile	289,110/748,795	14,800,000	Santiago	Spanish	South America
China	3,600,930/9,326,409	1,242,500,000	Beijing	Mandarin and local Chinese dialects	Asia
Colombia	401,040/1,038,694	38,600,000	Bogotá	Spanish	South America
Comoros	860/2,227	500,000	Moroni	French, Arabic, and Comoran	Africa
Congo Republic	131,850/341,492	2,700,000	Brazzaville	French, Kikongo, Lingala, and other African languages	Africa
Costa Rica	19,710/51,049	3,500,000	San José	Spanish and English	North America
Côte D'Ivoire (Ivory Coast)	122,780/318,000	15,600,000	Yamoussoukro	French and many African languages	Africa
Croatia	21,590/55,918	4,200,000	Zagreb	Serbo-Croatian	Europe
Cuba	42,400/109,816	11,100,000	Havana	Spanish	North America
Cyprus	3,568/9,242	700,000	Nicosia	Greek	Asia

Country	Area sq mi/sq km	Population	Capital	Major languages	Continent
Czech Republic	29,838/77,280	10,300,000	Prague	Czech and Slovak	Europe
Democratic Republic of Congo	875,309/2,267,050	49,000,000	Kinshasa	French, English, Swahili, Lingala, and other Bantu dialects	Africa
Denmark	16,320/42,269	5,300,000	Copenhagen	Danish and Faroese	Europe
Djibouti	8,950/23,181	700,000	Djibouti	Arabic and French	Africa
Dominica	290/751	100,000	Roseau	English and Creole	North America
Dominican Republic	18,680/48,381	8,300,000	Santo Domingo	Spanish	North America
Ecuador	106,890/276,845	12,200,000	Quito	Spanish and Quechua	South America
Egypt	384,444/995,450	65,500,000	Cairo	Arabic, English, and French	Africa
El Salvador	8,000/20,720	5,800,000	San Salvador	Spanish and Nahua	North America
Equatorial Guinea	10,830/28,050	400,000	Malabo	Spanish, Fang, and Bubi	Africa
Eritrea	38,996/101,000	3,800,000	Asmara	Tigrinya and Arabic	Africa
Estonia	16,320/42,269	1,400,000	Tallinn	Estonian, Latvian, Lithuanian, and Russian	Europe
Ethiopia	386,100/1,000,000	58,400,000	Addis Ababa	Amharic, English, and local languages	Africa
Fiji	7,054/18,270	800,000	Suva	Fijian, Hindi, and English	Islands in the Pacific Ocean
Finland	117,602/304,590	5,200,000	Helsinki	Finnish and Swedish	Europe
France	212,392/550,095	58,800,000	Paris	French	Europe
Gabon	99,490/257,679	1,200,000	Libreville	French, Fang, and Bantu dialects	Africa
Gambia	3,860/9,997	1,200,000	Banjul	English and Mandinka	Africa
Georgia	26,911/69,699	5,400,000	Tbilisi	Georgian and Russian	Asia
Germany	134,853/349,270	82,300,000	Berlin	German	Europe
Ghana	87,583/226,840	18,900,000	Accra	English and African languages	Africa

Country	Area (sq mi/sq km)	Population	Capital	Language	Continent
Greece	49,768/128,900	10,500,000	Athens	Greek	Europe
Grenada	130/337	100,000	St. George's	English and French patois	North America
Guatemala	41,860/108,417	11,600,000	Guatemala City	Spanish and Mayan dialects	North America
Guinea	94,873/245,721	7,500,000	Conakry	French, Soussou, and Manika	Africa
Guinea-Bissau	10,860/28,127	1,100,000	Bissau	Portuguese and Crioulo	Africa
Guyana	76,000/196,840	700,000	Georgetown	English, Hindi, and Urdu	South America
Haiti	10,640/27,558	7,500,000	Port-au-Prince	French and French Creole	North America
Honduras	43,200/111,888	5,900,000	Tegucigalpa	Spanish	North America
Hungary	35,363/92,431	10,100,000	Budapest	Hungarian	Europe
Iceland	38,707/100,251	300,000	Reykjavik	Icelandic	Europe
India	1,147,950/2,973,191	988,700,000	New Dehli	Hindi, English, and 14 other official languages	Asia
Indonesia	705,190/1,826,442	207,400,000	Jakarta	Bahasa	Asia
Iran	631,660/1,635,999	64,100,000	Tehran	Farsi, Turkic, and Kurdish	Asia
Iraq	168,870/437,373	21,800,000	Baghdad	Arabic and Kurdish	Asia
Ireland	26,598/68,890	3,700,000	Dublin	English and Irish	Europe
Israel	7,961/20,619	6,000,000	Jerusalem	Hebrew and Arabic	Asia
Italy	113,351/293,594	57,700,000	Rome	Italian	Europe
Jamaica	4,180/10,826	2,600,000	Kingston	English and Jamaican Creole	North America
Japan	145,370/376,508	126,400,000	Tokyo	Japanese	Asia
Jordan	34,336/88,930	4,600,000	Amman	Arabic	Asia
Kazakhstan	1,031,170/2,670,730	15,600,000	Almaty	Kazakh and Russian	Asia
Kenya	219,745/569,139	28,300,000	Nairobi	English and Swahili	Africa
Kiribati	313/811	82,449	Tarawa	Gilbertese and English	Islands in the Pacific Ocean
North Korea	46,490/120,409	22,200,000	Pyongyang	Korean	Asia
South Korea	38,120/98,731	46,400,000	Seoul	Korean	Asia

Country	Area sq mi/sq km	Population	Capital	Major languages	Continent
Kuwait	6,880/17,819	1,900,000	Kuwait City	Arabic	Asia
Kyrgyzstan	74,054/191,800	4,700,000	Bishkek	Kyrgyz and Russian	Asia
Laos	89,110/230,795	5,300,000	Vientiane	Lao, French, and English	Asia
Latvia	23,598/62,051	2,400,000	Riga	Latvian and English	Europe
Lebanon	3,950/10,231	4,100,000	Beirut	Arabic and French	Asia
Lesotho	11,720/30,355	2,100,000	Maseru	Sesotho and English	Africa
Liberia	37,190/96,322	2,800,000	Monrovia	English and Niger-Congo languages	Africa
Libya	679,360/1,759,542	5,700,000	Tripoli	Arabic, Italian, and English	Africa
Liechtenstein	60/155	30,000	Vaduz	German	Europe
Lithuania	25,019/64,799	3,700,000	Vilnius	Lithuanian, Russian, and Polish	Europe
Luxembourg	1,000/2,590	400,000	Luxembourg	Luxembourgisch, German, French, and English	Europe
Macedonia	9,819/25,431	2,000,000	Skopje	Macedonian	Europe
Madagascar	224,530/581,533	14,000,000	Antananarivo	French and Malagasy	Africa
Malawi	36,320/94,069	9,800,000	Lilongwe	English and Chichewa	Africa
Malaysia	126,850/328,542	22,200,000	Kuala Lumpur	Malay, English, and Chinese dialects	Asia
Maldives	116/300	300,000	Male	Divehi	Asia
Mali	471,120/1,220,201	10,100,000	Bamako	Bambura and French	Africa
Malta	120/311	400,000	Valletta	Maltese and English	Europe
Marshall Islands	70/181	100,000	Majuro	English, Marshallese dialects, and Japanese	Islands in the Pacific Ocean
Mauritania	395,840/1,025,226	2,500,000	Nouakchott	Arabic and Wolof	Africa
Mauritius	784/2,030	1,200,000	Port Louis	English, Creole, and French	Africa
Mexico	736,950/1,908,700	97,500,000	Mexico City	Spanish	North America

Country	Area (sq mi/sq km)	Population	Capital	Languages	Region
Micronesia	270/699	100,000	Palikir	English, Trukese, Yapese, and Kosrean	Islands in the Pacific Ocean
Moldova	12,730/32,971	4,200,000	Kishinev	Moldovan, Russian, and Gagauz	Europe
Monaco	.6/1.6	30,000	Monaco	French, Monégasque, and English	Europe
Mongolia	604,825/1,566,500	2,400,000	Ulaabaatar	Khalkha, Mongolian, Turkic, Russian, and Chinese	Asia
Morocco	173,320/446,309	28,600,000	Rabat	Arabic, Berber, and French	Africa
Mozambique	302,740/784,097	18,600,000	Maputo	Portuguese and African languages	Africa
Myanmar	253,880/657,549	47,100,000	Yangon	Burmese	Asia
Namibia	317,870/823,283	1,600,000	Windhoek	English, Afrikaans, and German	Africa
Nauru	21/54	10,390	Yaren	Nauruan and English	Islands in the Pacific Ocean
Nepal	52,820/136,804	23,700,000	Kathmandu	Nepali	Asia
Netherlands	13,097/33,921	15,700,000	Amsterdam	Dutch	Europe
New Zealand	103,420/267,987	3,800,000	Wellington	English and Maori	Islands in the Pacific Ocean
Nicaragua	46,873/121,401	4,800,000	Managua	Spanish	North America
Niger	489,070/1,266,691	10,100,000	Niamey	French, Hausa, and Djerma	Africa
Nigeria	351,650/910,774	121,800,000	Abuja	English, Hausa, Yoruba, Ibo, and Fulani	Africa
Norway	118,467/306,830	4,400,000	Oslo	Norwegian	Europe
Oman	82,030/212,458	2,500,000	Muscat	Arabic	Asia
Pakistan	297,640/770,888	141,900,000	Islamabad	Urdu, Punjabi, and English	Asia
Palau	190/492	20,000	Koror	Palauan and English	Islands in the Pacific Ocean
Panama	28,737/74,428	2,800,000	Panama City	Spanish and English	North America
Papua New Guinea	174,850/452,862	4,300,000	Port Moresby	Pidgin English, English, and Motu	Islands in the Pacific Ocean
Paraguay	153,400/397,306	5,200,000	Asunción	Spanish and Guarani	South America
Peru	494,210/1,280,044	26,100,000	Lima	Spanish, Quechua, and Aymará	South America
Philippines	115,120/298,161	75,300,000	Manila	Filipino, Tagalog, and English	Asia

Country	Area sq mi/sq km	Population	Capital	Major languages	Continent
Poland	117,537/304,420	38,700,000	Warsaw	Polish	Europe
Portugal	35,502/91,950	10,000,000	Lisbon	Portuguese	Europe
Qatar	4,250/11,008	500,000	Doha	Arabic and English	Asia
Romania	88,934/230,339	22,500,000	Bucharest	Romanian, Hungarian, and German	Europe
Russia	6,520,656/16,888,499	147,000,000	Moscow	Russian	Europe and Asia
Rwanda	9,525/24,670	8,000,000	Kigali	Kinyarwanda, French, and Kiswahili	Africa
St. Kitts and Nevis	140/363	40,000	Basseterre	English	North America
St. Lucia	236/611	100,000	Castries	English and French patois	North America
St. Vincent and the Grenadines	150/389	100,000	Kingstown	English	North America
Samoa	1,090/2,823	200,000	Apia	Samoan and English	Islands in the Pacific Ocean
San Marino	20/52	20,000	San Marino	Italian	Europe
São Tomé and Principe	293/759	200,000	São Tomé	Portuguese	Africa
Saudi Arabia	830,000/2,149,700	20,200,000	Riyadh	Arabic	Asia
Senegal	74,340/192,541	9,000,000	Dakar	French and Wolof	Africa
Seychelles	174/451	100,000	Victoria	Creole, English, and French	Africa
Sierra Leone	27,650/71,614	4,600,000	Freetown	English, Mende, Temne, and Krio	Africa
Singapore	236/611	3,900,000	Singapore	Chinese, English, Malay and Tamil	Asia
Slovakia	18,564/48,080	5,400,000	Bratislava	Slovak and Hungarian	Europe
Slovenia	7,768/20,119	2,000,000	Ljubljana	Slovenian	Europe
Solomon Islands	10,810/27,998	400,000	Honiara	English, Pidgin English, and Melanesian	Islands in the Pacific Ocean
Somalia	242,220/627,350	10,700,000	Mogadishu	Somali and Arabic	Africa
South Africa	471,440/1,221,030	38,900,000	Pretoria, Cape Town, and Bloemfontein	Afrikaans, English, Zulu, and other African languages	Africa

Country	Area (sq mi/sq km)	Population	Capital	Languages	Continent
Spain	192,834/499,440	39,400,000	Madrid	Spanish and Catalan	Europe
Sri Lanka	24,950/64,621	18,900,000	Colombo	Sinhala, Tamil, and English	Asia
Sudan	917,375/2,376,000	28,500,000	Khartoum	Arabic, Nubian, and Sudanic languages	Africa
Suriname	60,230/155,996	400,000	Paramaribo	Dutch, English, and Hindi	South America
Swaziland	6,640/17,198	1,000,000	Mbabane	Siswati and English	Africa
Sweden	158,927/411,621	8,900,000	Stockholm	Swedish	Europe
Switzerland	15,270/39,590	7,100,000	Bern	German, French, Italian, and Romansch	Europe
Syria	70,958/183,781	15,600,000	Damascus	Arabic and Kurdish	Asia
Taiwan	13,970/36,182	21,700,000	Taipei	Mandarin, Taiwanese, and Hakka dialects	Asia
Tajikistan	54,286/140,601	6,100,000	Dushanbe	Tajik and Russian	Asia
Tanzania	341,154/883,588	30,600,000	Dar es Salaam	Swahili and English	Africa
Thailand	197,250/510,878	61,100,000	Bangkok	Thai and English	Asia
Togo	21,000/54,390	4,900,000	Lomé	French, Kabye, Ewe, Mina, and Dagomba	Africa
Tonga	290/751	107,335	Nuku'alofa	Tongan and English	Islands in the Pacific Ocean
Trinidad and Tobago	1,980/5,128	1,300,000	Port-of-Spain	English, Hindi, and French	North America
Tunisia	59,980/155,348	9,500,000	Tunis	Arabic and French	Africa
Turkey	297,150/769,619	64,800,000	Ankara	Turkish, Kurdish, and Arabic	Asia and Europe
Turkmenistan	181,440/470,000	4,700,000	Ashgabat	Turkmen, Russian, and Uzbek	Asia
Tuvalu	9/23	10,297	Funafuti	Tuvaluan and English	Islands in the Pacific Ocean
Uganda	77,085/199,650	21,000,000	Kampala	English, Luganda, Swahili, and Bantu languages	Africa
Ukraine	223,687/579,349	50,300,000	Kiev	Ukranian, Russian, Romanian, and Polish	Europe

Country	Area sq mi/sq km	Population	Capital	Major languages	Continent
United Arab Emirates	32,280/83,605	2,700,000	Abu Dhabi	Arabic, Persian, English, Hindi, and Urdu	Asia
United Kingdom	93,282/241,600	59,100,000	London	English, Welsh, and Scottish Gaelic	Europe
United States	3,536,340/9,159,121	270,200,000	Washington, D.C.	English and Spanish	North America
Uruguay	67,490/174,499	3,200,000	Montevideo	Spanish and Brazilero	South America
Uzbekistan	159,938/414,356	24,100,000	Tashkent	Uzbek, Russian, and Tajik	Asia
Vanuatu	4,710/12,199	200,000	Port-Vila	Bislama, English, and French	Islands in the Pacific Ocean
Vatican City (The Holy See)	.2/.4	1,000	Vatican City	Italian and Latin	Europe
Venezuela	340,560/882,050	23,300,000	Caracas	Spanish and Indian dialects	South America
Vietnam	126,670/325,485	78,500,000	Hanoi	Vietnamese, French, Chinese, English, and Khmer	Asia
Yemen	203,850/527,972	15,800,000	San'a	Arabic	Asia
Yugoslavia	39,382/102,000	10,600,000	Belgrade	Serbo-Croatian and Albanian	Europe
Zambia	287,020/743,382	9,500,000	Lusaka	English and about 70 Bantu dialects	Africa
Zimbabwe	149,363/386,850	11,000,000	Harare	English, Shona, and Sindebele	Africa

Presidents of the United States

No.	President (birth and death dates)	Term(s)	Party	Vice President(s)
1	George Washington (1732–1799)	1789–1797		John Adams
2	John Adams (1735–1826)	1797–1801	Federalist	Thomas Jefferson
3	Thomas Jefferson (1743–1826)	1801–1809	Democratic-Republican	Aaron Burr George Clinton
4	James Madison (1751–1836)	1809–1817	Democratic-Republican	George Clinton Elbridge Gerry
5	James Monroe (1758–1831)	1817–1825	Democratic-Republican	Daniel D. Tompkins
6	John Quincy Adams (1767–1848)	1825–1829	Democratic-Republican	John C. Calhoun
7	Andrew Jackson (1767–1845)	1829–1837	Democratic	John C. Calhoun Martin Van Buren
8	Martin Van Buren (1782–1862)	1837–1841	Democratic	Richard M. Johnson
9	William H. Harrison (1773–1841)	1841	Whig	John Tyler
10	John Tyler (1790–1862)	1841–1845	Whig	None
11	James K. Polk (1795–1849)	1845–1849	Democratic	George M. Dallas
12	Zachary Taylor (1784–1850)	1849–1850	Whig	Millard Fillmore
13	Millard Fillmore (1800–1874)	1850–1853	Whig	None
14	Franklin Pierce (1804–1869)	1853–1857	Democratic	William R. King
15	James Buchanan (1791–1868)	1857–1861	Democratic	John C. Breckinridge

No.	President (birth and death dates)	Term(s)	Party	Vice President(s)
16	Abraham Lincoln (1809–1865)	1861–1865	Republican	Hannibal Hamlin Andrew Johnson
17	Andrew Johnson (1808–1875)	1865–1869	Republican	None
18	Ulysses S. Grant (1822–1885)	1869–1877	Republican	Schuyler Colfax Henry Wilson
19	Rutherford B. Hayes (1822–1893)	1877–1881	Republican	William A. Wheeler
20	James A. Garfield (1831–1881)	1881	Republican	Chester A. Arthur
21	Chester A. Arthur (1830–1886)	1881–1885	Republican	None
22 24	Grover Cleveland (1837–1908)	1885–1889 1893–1897	Democratic	Thomas A. Hendricks Adlai E. Stevenson
23	Benjamin Harrison (1833–1901)	1889–1893	Republican	Levi P. Morton
25	William McKinley (1843–1901)	1897–1901	Republican	Garret Hobart Theodore Roosevelt
26	Theodore Roosevelt (1858–1919)	1901–1909	Republican	Charles W. Fairbanks
27	William H. Taft (1857–1930)	1909–1913	Republican	James S. Sherman
28	Woodrow Wilson (1856–1924)	1913–1921	Democratic	Thomas R. Marshall
29	Warren G. Harding (1865–1923)	1921–1923	Republican	Calvin Coolidge
30	Calvin Coolidge (1872–1933)	1923–1929	Republican	Charles G. Dawes
31	Herbert C. Hoover (1874–1964)	1929–1933	Republican	Charles Curtis
32	Franklin D. Roosevelt (1882–1945)	1933–1945	Democrat	John N. Garner Henry A. Wallace Harry S Truman
33	Harry S Truman (1884–1972)	1945–1953	Democrat	Alben W. Barkley

No.	President (birth and death dates)	Term(s)	Party	Vice President(s)
34	Dwight D. Eisenhower (1890–1969)	1953–1961	Republican	Richard M. Nixon
35	John F. Kennedy (1917–1963)	1961–1963	Democrat	Lyndon B. Johnson
36	Lyndon B. Johnson (1908–1973)	1963–1969	Democrat	Hubert H. Humphrey
37	Richard M. Nixon (1913–1994)	1969–1974	Republican	Spiro T. Agnew Gerald R. Ford
38	Gerald R. Ford (1913–)	1974–1977	Republican	Nelson A. Rockefeller
39	James E. Carter (1924–)	1977–1981	Democrat	Walter F. Mondale
40	Ronald W. Reagan (1911–)	1981–1989	Republican	George H. Bush
41	George H. Bush (1924–)	1989–1993	Republican	J. Danforth Quayle
42	William Jefferson Clinton (1946–)	1993–2001	Democrat	Albert Gore, Jr.
43	George W. Bush (1946–)	2001–	Republican	Richard B. Cheney

Useful Web Sites

These Web sites for social studies and for writing get good reviews. Most of them are *not* designed for students below college level, but they are all worth visiting.

Geography

Association of American Geographers
www.aag.org
This gives you a chance to see what matters to professional geographers.

INFOMINE: Maps
http://infomine.ucr.edu/cgi-bin/search?maps
This is a place to examine catalogs of maps.

Colorado University: Resources for Geographers
www.Colorado.edu/geography/virtdept/resources/contents.htm
Here's another site with map collections.

Rand McNally
www.randmcnally.com/home/
You can examine here an Internet atlas from the mapmaker to the world.

Government

Political Science Resources on the Web
www.lib.umich.edu/libhome/Documents.center/polisci.html
This site provides resources for teachers and students doing research in government and related fields.

Richard Kimber's Political Science Resources
www.psr.keele.ac.uk
This is the place where you should be able to find material about current elections and information about national and local governments.

History

Center for History and New Media
http://chnm.gmu.edu
This site is a good place to begin looking for history resources on the Web.

Douglass: Archives of American Public Address
http://douglass.speech.nwu.edu
This source of American historical information belongs to Northwestern University.

Horus' History Links
www.ucr.edu/h-gig/horuslinks.html
This site belongs to the Department of History at the University of California, Riverside campus.

Internet Resources in History
www.tntech.edu/www/acad/hist/resources.html
Another academic site—this time, one that belongs to Tennessee
    Technological University.

WWW-VL History Index
http://history.cc.ukans.edu/history/VL
The advantage of this site is that it classifies resources according to country
    or region.

Writing

Almanac Online
www.infoplease.com
Search by topic, and view articles one at a time.

Grammar, Usage, and Style
www.refdesk.com/factgram.html
This site provides hundreds of links to sites that can help with editing.

Online Resources for Writers
http://webster.commnet.edu/writing/writing.htm
Yet another way to find links to reference tools and to help with grammar.

Research Tools for Writers
www.encyclopedia.com
This site offers many products for sale but also provides encyclopedia entries
    for free.

Preamble to the Constitution of the United States (1789)

We the People of the United States, in order to form a more perfect Union, establish Justice, insure domestic tranquility, provide for the common defense, promote the general Welfare, and secure the Blessing of Liberty to ourselves and our Posterity, do ordain and establish this Constitution for the United States of America.

Bill of Rights (1791)

Amendment 1. Freedom of Religion, Speech, Press, Assembly, and Petition

Congress shall make no law respecting an establishment of religion, or prohibiting the free exercise thereof; or abridging the freedom of speech, or of the press; or the right of the people peaceably to assemble, and to petition the government for a redress of grievances.

Amendment 2. Right to Keep Weapons

A well-regulated militia, being necessary to the security of a free state, the right of the people to keep and bear arms shall not be infringed.

Amendment 3. Protection Against Quartering Soldiers

No soldier shall, in time of peace, be quartered in any house, without the consent of the owner, nor in time of war, but in a manner prescribed by law.

Amendment 4. Freedom from Unreasonable Search and Seizure

The right of the people to be secure in their persons, house, papers, and effects, against unreasonable searches and seizures, shall not be violated, and no warrants shall issue, but upon probable cause, supported by oath or affirmation, and particularly describing the place to be searched, and the persons or things to be seized.

Amendment 5. Rights of Persons Accused of a Crime

No person shall be held to answer for a capital, or otherwise infamous, crime, unless on a presentment or indictment of a grand jury, except in cases arising in the land or naval forces, or in the militia, when in actual service in time of war or public danger; nor shall any person be subject for the same offense to be twice put in jeopardy of life or limb; nor shall be compelled in any criminal case to be a witness against himself, nor to be deprived of life, liberty, or property, without due process of law; nor shall private property be taken for public use, without just compensation.

Amendment 6. Right to a Jury Trial in Criminal Cases

In all criminal prosecutions, the accused shall enjoy the right to a speedy and public trial, by an impartial jury of the state and district wherein the crime shall have been committed, which district shall have been previously ascertained by law, and to be informed of the nature and cause of the accusation; to be confronted with the witnesses against him; to have compulsory process for obtaining witnesses in his favor, and to have the assistance of counsel for his defense.

Amendment 7. Right to a Jury Trial in Civil Cases

In suits at common law, where the value in controversy shall exceed twenty dollars, the right of trial by jury shall be preserved, and no fact tried by a jury shall be otherwise re-examined in any court of the United States than according to the rules of the common law.

Amendment 8. Protection from Unfair Fines and Punishment

Excessive bail should not be required, nor excessive fines imposed, nor cruel and unusual punishments inflicted.

Amendment 9. Other Rights of the People

The enumeration in the Constitution, of certain rights, shall not be construed to deny or disparage others retained by the people.

Amendment 10. Powers of the States and the People

The powers not delegated to the United States by the Constitution, nor prohibited by its states, are reserved to the states respectively, or to the people.

Declaration of Independence (1776)

When in the Course of human events it becomes necessary for one people to dissolve the political bands which have connected them and to assume among the powers of the earth the separate and equal station to which the Laws of Nature and of Nature's God entitle them, a decent respect to the opinions of mankind requires that they should declare the causes which impel them to the separation.

We hold these truths to be self-evident: that all men are created equal; that they are endowed by their Creator with certain unalienable Rights; that among these are Life, Liberty and the pursuit of Happiness; That to secure these rights, Governments are instituted among Men, deriving their just powers from the consent of the governed; That whenever any Form of Government becomes destructive of these ends, it is the Right of the People to alter or to abolish it, and to institute new Government, laying its foundation on such principles, and organizing its powers in such form, as to them shall seem most likely to effect their Safety and Happiness. Prudence, indeed, will dictate that Governments long established should not be changed for light and transient causes; and accordingly all experience hath shown that mankind are more disposed to suffer while evils are sufferable than to right themselves by abolishing the forms to which they are accustomed. But when a long train of abuses and usurpations, pursuing invariably the same Objects, evinces a design to reduce them under absolute Despotism, it is their right, it is their duty, to throw off such Government, and to provide new Guards for their future security. Such has been the patient sufferance of these Colonies; and such is now the necessity which constrains them to alter their former Systems of Government. The history of the present King of Great Britain is a history of repeated injuries and usurpations, all having in direct object the establishment of an absolute Tyranny over the States. To prove this, let Facts be submitted to a candid world.

He has refused his Assent to Laws the most wholesome and necessary for the public good.

He has forbidden his Governors to pass Laws of immediate and pressing importance, unless suspended in their operation till his Assent should be obtained; and when so suspended, he has utterly neglected to attend to them.

He has refused to pass other Laws for the accommodation of large districts of people, unless these people would relinquish the right of Representation in the Legislature, a right inestimable to them and formidable to tyrants only.

He has called together legislative bodies at places unusual, uncomfortable, and distant from the depository of their public records, for the sole purpose of fatiguing them into compliance with his measures.

He has dissolved Representative Houses repeatedly, for opposing with manly firmness his invasions on the right of the people.

He has refused for a long time after such dissolutions to cause others to be elected, whereby the Legislative powers, incapable of Annihilation, have returned to the People at large for their exercise, the State remaining in the mean time exposed to all the dangers of invasions from without and convulsions within.

He has endeavored to prevent the population of these States; for that purpose obstructing the Laws for Naturalization of Foreigners, refusing to pass others to encourage their migration hither, and raising the conditions of new Appropriations of Lands.

He has obstructed the Administration of Justice, by refusing his Assent to Laws for establishing Judiciary powers.

He has made Judges dependent on his Will alone for the tenure of their offices, and the amount of their salaries.

He has erected a multitude of New Offices, and sent hither swarms of Officers to harass our people and eat out their substance.

He has kept among us, in times of peace, Standing Armies, without the Consent of our legislatures.

He has affected to render the Military independent of, and superior to, the Civil power.

He has combined with others to subject us to a jurisdiction foreign to our constitution and unacknowledged by our laws; giving his Assent to their Acts of pretended Legislation:

For quartering large bodies of armed troops among us;

For protecting them, by a mock Trial, from punishment for any murders which they should commit on the Inhabitants of these States;

For cutting off our Trade with parts of the world;

For imposing Taxes on us without our Consent;

For depriving us, in many cases, of the benefits of Trial by Jury;

For transporting us beyond Seas to be tried for pretended offenses;

For abolishing the free System of English Laws in a neighboring Province, establishing therein an Arbitrary government, and enlarging its boundaries, so as to render it at once an example and fit instrument for introducing the same absolute rule into these Colonies;

For taking away our Charters, abolishing our most valuable Laws, and altering, fundamentally, the Forms of our Governments;

For suspending our own Legislatures, and declaring themselves invested with Power to legislate for us in all cases whatsoever.

He has abdicated Government here, by declaring us out of his Protection and waging War against us.

He has plundered our seas, ravaged our Coasts, burned our towns, and destroyed the lives of our people.

He is at this time transporting large Armies of foreign Mercenaries to complete the works of death, desolation and tyranny, already begun with circumstances of Cruelty and perfidy scarcely paralleled in the most barbarous ages, and totally unworthy the Head of a civilized nation.

He has constrained our fellow Citizens taken on the high Seas to bear Arms against their Country, to become the executioners of their friends and Brethren, or to fall themselves by their Hands.

He has excited domestic insurrections amongst us, and has endeavored to bring on the inhabitants of our frontiers the merciless Indian Savages whose known rule of warfare is an undistinguished destruction of all ages, sexes, and conditions.

In every stage of these Oppressions We have Petitioned for Redress in the most humble terms. Our repeated Petitions have been answered only by repeated injury. A Prince whose character is thus marked by every act which may define a Tyrant is unfit to be the ruler of a free people.

Nor have We been wanting in attentions to our British Brethren. We have warned them from time to time of attempts by their legislature to extend an unwarrantable jurisdiction over us. We have reminded them of the circumstances of our emigration and settlement here. We have appealed to their native justice and magnanimity, and we have conjured them by the ties of our common kindred to disavow these usurpations, which would inevitably interrupt our connections and correspondence. They too have been deaf to the voice of justice and consanguinity. We must therefore acquiesce in the necessity which denounces our Separation and hold them, as we hold the rest of mankind, Enemies in War, in Peace Friends.

We, therefore, the Representatives of the United States of America in General Congress Assembled, appealing to the Supreme Judge of the world for the rectitude of our intentions, do in the Name and by the Authority of the good people of these Colonies, solemnly publish and declare that these United Colonies are and of right ought to be Free and Independent States; that they are Absolved from all Allegiance to the British Crown, and that all political connection between them and the State of Great Britain is and ought to be totally dissolved, and that as Free and Independent States, they have full Power to levy War, conclude Peace, contract Alliance, establish Commerce, and to do all other Acts and Things which Independent States may of right do.

And for the support of this Declaration, with a firm reliance on the protection of Divine Providence, we mutually pledge to each other our Lives, our Fortunes, and our sacred Honor.

Project-Scheduling Forms

Scheduling a Book Report

Use this form or modify it to fit your assignment and your teacher's expectations.

Task	Try to finish by
1. Choose a book for a book report, and get it approved if necessary.	_____
2. Finish reading the book and taking notes.	_____
3. Organize the notes.	_____
4. Write an outline.	_____
5. Write a first draft.	
Write the opener.	_____
Write the body.	_____
Write the conclusion.	_____
(You do not have to do these three tasks in order.)	
6. Make up a title for the book report.	_____
7. Use the "Checklist for Evaluating" on page 45.	_____
8. Troubleshoot the first draft on your own (revise, edit, proofread).	_____
9. Get feedback from another reader.	_____
10. Write final draft (proofread again).	_____

Scheduling a Research Report

Use this form or modify it to fit your assignment and your teacher's expectations.

Stage	Try to finish by
1. Get a topic, and get it approved if necessary.	_____
2. Find and evaluate sources (you will generate research questions during this stage).	_____
3. Keep track of sources (use "How to List Sources" on pages 57–58).	_____
4. Take notes from sources.	_____
5. Decide on a presentation (your teacher may decide for you).	_____
6. Organize your notes.	_____
7. Write an outline.	_____
8. Write a first draft.	_____
9. Make up a title for the research report.	_____
10. List sources.	_____
11. Fix the research report by troubleshooting (revising, editing, and proofreading). Also get feedback from another reader.	_____
12. Write the final draft (proofread again).	_____

121

Idea Organizers

Idea Organizer 1: Flowchart

Use a flowchart like this one to keep track of events in the order in which they happen. You can add more rectangles if necessary.

Idea Organizer 2: Cluster

Use a cluster diagram to help you brainstorm. (A cluster is sometimes called a map or a web.) Write your main idea or topic in the middle circle. Then fill in the outer circles with details that support the main idea or that relate to the topic. Add more outer circles as necessary.

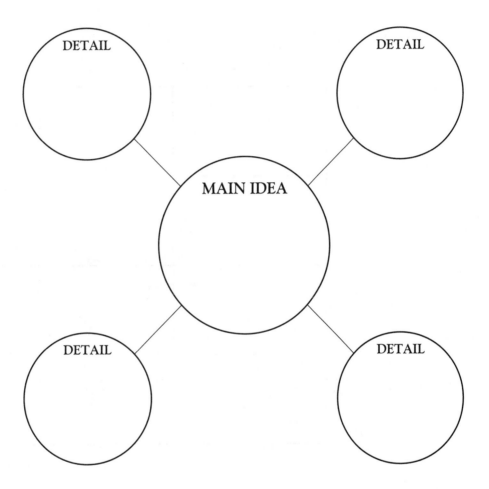

Idea Organizer 3: Column Chart

Use a chart made up of columns to organize information. You may need fewer or more columns, depending on the assignment. Three columns would work nicely if the assignment asks you, for example, to describe three things about a famous person—say, his or her appearance, accomplishments, and famous sayings. You may also add or remove rows.

Idea Organizer 4: Venn Diagram

A diagram of overlapping circles can help when you have to compare and contrast two people, places, objects, or events—say, the American Revolution and the French Revolution. Write the first item on the line in the left circle and the second item on the line in the right circle. Under the lines, list things about each item that are different—for example, how the immediate results of each revolution differed. Under the word "SAME," list things about the two items that are similar—for example, when the two revolutions took place.

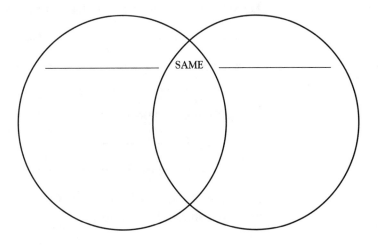

Self-Evaluation of Student Writing

Writers should feel free to modify the list of questions to fit their own style of working and their own strengths and weaknesses as writers.

What do I like the most about this piece of writing? Why?

_____

_____

Have I made my main point clear? If not, what can I do to make it clear?

_____

_____

Have I supported, or backed up, my main point with enough proof or details? If not, what do I have to add?

_____

_____

Have I repeated myself (and bored the reader)? If so, what should I take out, and what should I put in its place?

_____

_____

Have I included details that really don't belong? Should I change my main idea, or should I take out the details that don't belong?

_____

_____

Is my piece of writing easy to follow? If not, what can I do to help the reader get through it?

_____

_____

How are my spelling, punctuation, and language? (Agreement? Pronoun reference? Pronoun case? Placement of modifiers? Verb forms?)

_____

_____

INDEX